WALKING EACH OTHER HOME

SPIRITUAL COMPANIONSHIP FOR DEMENTIA CAREGIVERS

JEAN M. DENTON

Morehouse Publishing
NEW YORK

Morehouse Publishing, 19 East 34th Street, New York, NY 10016

Morehouse Publishing is an imprint of Church Publishing Incorporated.

Cover art and design by Gillian Whiting
Typeset by PerfecType, Nashville, Tennessee

Library of Congress Cataloging-in-Publication Data

Names: Denton, Jean (Jean Margaret), author.
Title: Walking each other home : spiritual companionship for dementia
   caregivers / Jean M. Denton.
Description: New York, NY : Morehouse Publishing, 2021.
Identifiers: LCCN 2021015992 (print) | LCCN 2021015993 (ebook) | ISBN
   9781640654150 (paperback) | ISBN 9781640654167 (epub)
Subjects: LCSH: Caregivers--Religious life. | Dementia--Patients--Care. |
   Dementia--Religious aspects--Christianity.
Classification: LCC BV4910.9 .D46 2021 (print) | LCC BV4910.9 (ebook) |
   DDC 248.8/616831--dc23
LC record available at https://lccn.loc.gov/2021015992
LC ebook record available at https://lccn.loc.gov/2021015993

For Tom, in absentia,
and
For all who have supported Tom and me in our long walk
and
For dementia caregivers everywhere

Contents

Part Five: "Are We There Yet?"

Preface

You might ask if we need yet another book about dementia. Many memoirs have been written with great tenderness honoring a loved one who has died from this mind-stealing disease. You can find poignant stories written in the voice of a person with dementia, telling what dementia is like from the inside. A great library of books is available to educate dementia caregivers about practical issues.

So why did I write this book?

I wrote because something significant was missing—something to do with spirit. Although some books acknowledge that dementia caregivers have spiritual needs, they rarely go beyond giving those needs a passing nod as the reader is directed to their religious upbringing. Not all people have a religious upbringing; for some who do, their early religious training may no longer be useful. The guidance offered in caregiving guidebooks is, unfortunately, too often superficial and is couched as self-care that would allow us to continue giving care rather than offering true care for our souls. Caregivers have spiritual needs intrinsic to all human beings. We have increased needs because we have taken on an enormous and often hidden role. Spiritual concerns (anger, loneliness, guilt, and hope) change over years of dementia caregiving as the disease landscape changes. New feelings and thoughts arise. These are serious matters that often aren't taken seriously enough. This book is an effort to begin addressing these matters.

I also wrote this book to remember Tom, my much-loved partner and husband of twenty years. Thirteen of those years were spent walking with Tom's younger-onset Alzheimer's. To "re-member" Tom means putting together again the parts of him and making him whole again in my heart. I don't want to lose him or the gifts that our life together gave me.

I also wrote hoping to find meaning in my years of dementia care-giving, a time when my professional options were constricted and my personal goals were put on hold. I often asked, "Why? What is the meaning in this? Why does a good God let a man suffer the indignity of losing his very self?" I struggled to find a way through the morass of feelings and questions. If what I learned can help lighten others' struggles, this book will have been well worth the effort. Since I am a registered nurse, a spiritual director, and an ordained priest, Tom often teased that we had all the bases covered, but one never does. There's always something new to learn, and I was often a reluctant learner,

My aim is to walk with you for a while on your journey and help you articulate your own spiritual story. As you explore what is true, what is not, what gives you purpose, and what keeps you caring, you will be mining gold.

Introduction

T he thirteenth-century Turkish satirist and trickster Nasreddin Hodja told wonderfully provocative stories. Oral folk tradition has passed them down through the centuries and they are still told to children today. One of his stories is especially fitting to dementia caregivers as we seek to find the meaning of our experience. It goes like this:

> One night, Nasreddin was found by one of his followers searching under a streetlight. The follower asked, "Master, what are you doing?" Nasreddin responded that he was searching for his key. The follower joined in and eventually asked, "Where did you drop it?" Nasreddin replied, "Over there in the shadows," pointing to a spot several yards away. "But why aren't you looking over there?" "Because there is more light here," the master replied.[1]

The question of where to search for the key—where the light is best or where it has been dropped—may seem easy to answer, yet to step into the shadows is difficult. An ill-defined world where shapes shift demands a change from seeing clearly to sensing. This book will take you into the shadows, into dark, uncomfortable places. Searching for meaning here is not for the faint-hearted, but dementia caregivers are not a withering group.

The light that is shined on dementia caregiving is usually for the benefit of the person being cared for. It's obvious that people who carry dementia within their own bodies warrant as much light as possible—stalwart support, excellent research, and empathetic clinical care. I would not begin to compare our losses to those of people who literally lose their minds, but seeing our needs as only relating to the person for whom we care is limited and limiting. Too often we are not seen whole. Are we not just as human? Are our issues not also in need of attention? Are we not more than functionaries whose sole purpose in living is to care for one other who is terminally ill? Dementia changes us too: our inner being and even our bodies. We are too often a forgotten lot, and this writing seeks to change that.

What You Will Find in This Book

You will meet Tom, my husband and best friend. Our thirteen-year odyssey of younger-onset dementia is naturally unique to us. Your journey is your own, just as your loved one's dementia is not like that of any other. That said, I believe the poet Maya Angelou who wrote, "We are more alike, my friends, than we are unalike."[2] I believe we would do well to travel together as much as we can on this long and challenging journey.

You will meet me in this book, and I hope you will find in me an experienced companion, one who has compassion for others on the journey. I struggled with language to describe my experience and decided to call it dementia caregiving. I could have used other words (*care partner, caregiver to a person with memory loss*), but I decided on a commonly used phrase for consistency. Also, I use the word *dementia* knowing it is not one disease but multiple clinical processes with diverse causes. Some people find the word *dementia* offensive, but it is accurate. I chose to do my part to redeem the word.

If my goal is achieved, you will meet yourself in this book. I invite you to explore your own feelings and responses to what I share. We each develop our own meaning (even our own theology) as we encounter spiritual issues along this path. No one has "the" answers to spiritual questions, but each of us has our own hard-earned knowledge, our own valid perspective, and our own truthful understandings. The answers we find may change with time and more experience, but they remain our unique answers.

How This Book Is Organized

The book is divided into five parts:

- Part One: "Starting the Long Walk" introduces Tom and me as traveling companions, identifies dementia caregiver needs as the experts see them, and considers what it means to care. What is care, anyway? How is it valued, and by whom? Caring is a word and concept we seldom take time to examine.

- Part Two: "Companions" identifies your walking partners. No one goes on this risky journey alone. Your most intimate companion is the one for whom you care, but there are others. You walk with other dementia caregivers, most of whom are unknown to you. They are, nonetheless, very real companions on the very same journey. You also walk with your God, the One who has many names, based on your understanding and experience of the divine. Your original image of God was likely formed in your youth and either developed or discarded as you matured. We each carry a sense of the numinous, the "beyond."

- Part Three: "Provisions for the Journey" offers nourishment for you along the way. I'll share my perspective on prayer for your reflection. I'll suggest some spiritual practices to support you for the long haul. These are not esoteric or foreign practices, but simple things that you might actually be able to fit into your overloaded day. Because the feelings you encounter can be confusing, I offer the concept of the *mandorla* as a way of handling contradictory feelings.

- Part Four: "Encounters along the Way" is a collection of possible feelings and experiences we confront in dementia caregiving. The encounters are not sequential, nor are these chapters necessarily meant to be read in any particular order. Rather, one day you may experience helplessness and want to explore that chapter. Another time, you might find your anger welling up and seek to explore that. Go where you are led on any given day. I make no claim that the encounters I have identified are experienced by all dementia caregivers, nor do I see this list as comprehensive. My hope is that they will offer touchstones, a form of companionship to my fellow caregivers. "Encounters along the Way" may be where this book can be most valuable. It is where growth will come. You are invited to explore your own experiences in dementia caregiving and see them in a fuller way. By reflecting, you will be able to put yourself into this book. Your book will be written by you. I don't have the last word; you do. I don't have your answers, but you do, and they live inside your deepest self.

- Part Five: "Are We There Yet?" offers a conclusion that really is no conclusion. We will always carry memories and questions about the meaning of dementia and dementia caregiving. It's a part of our continuing spiritual growth.

What You Will Need to Use This Book

A Way to Record Your Thoughts

What I have written is intended to provoke you to think about your own caregiving experience, hopefully integrating diverse threads. Recording your thoughts can take different forms, like journaling or expressive art or recording your voice.

Reflecting on your experiences can help you rise above the daily grind. Getting ideas out of your head clears your mind of its endless, often circular, chattering about an issue. Mental blathering is silenced by the light of loving reflection. When we name feelings, they are out there in front of us; they can no longer lurk below consciousness or hide behind busyness. They become more real and also more pliable. Something can be done with them: they can be met, explored, sorted, and related to other feelings. They can be better understood, even embraced.

If you are journaling, you will want to invest in a blank book that you find attractive. It could be a spiral-bound notebook or a hardbound journal—whatever pleases you. Find a pen or pencil that feels good to your hand. Or use an electronic tool if that's preferable. Not everyone— and in particular dementia caregivers—can make time to do "proper" journaling. Instead of thoughtful paragraphs, maybe there is time only to jot down a few thoughts. Maybe all you can manage is one-word bullet points. At least these will leave a trail of your reflections. Later you can revisit the notes and expand on them if you like.

Not everyone enjoys using words. Maybe a collage is your way of tracking what's going on inside you. Your tool might be clay, colored pencils, or another medium. Any of these can be the means of getting your inner experience out into the light. Use whatever suits your time and inclinations. Gather the tools that you'll need and store them in a place where you can access them without having to assemble them each time you want to use them.

Recording your experience is personal, helping you to hear and see yourself. No one else is listening or watching; your reflections are yours and yours alone. You need safety in order to be honest and vulnerable. Your reflections don't have to be well constructed or thoroughly formed. They don't need to be clear. They only need to be true and real.

A Bit of Time

Time, of course, is that all too scarce commodity. It doesn't have to be a lot of time; maybe ten or twenty minutes. The time needn't be rigidly set, and it can be taken intermittently when you find it. On the other hand, it might be a regular appointment you have with yourself, marked on your calendar as you would a doctor's appointment. If you have respite care for a day, you might want to take yourself to a quiet place and really delve in. Use what time you can afford. How I wish I could give you more time in your overly packed day, but each of us gets just twenty-four hours each and every day, no matter what demands are put on our time. It is ultimately our choice as to how to spend them.

A Curiosity

You'll need to foster a curiosity about yourself and your experience of dementia caregiving. You'll be thinking as well as feeling. Curiosity requires a willingness to step back and to take a long, loving look at your life. This curiosity is an investment in yourself and a way to honor your experience.

An Openness to Difficult Feelings

This is the hardest part: welcoming the parts of life that hurt. Our minds are programmed to hide from us the things we don't want to face. When they crop up, we push the feelings away, hoping they will die from neglect. But our rational, thinking selves know they won't disappear. They will smolder and erupt into flames when we least want or expect them. Take courage; remember that anxiety is only increased by not wanting to feel what we feel. The pain is worth the effort. Remember too that feelings are embodied. Whatever is going around in your head is also going around in your body. Listen to your body.

Practically Speaking

These guidelines will support your reflection.

- Choose a place you find comfortable—a favorite chair or a place near the light from a window.
- Quiet yourself with some consciously deep breaths to help empty your mind. Offer a short affirmation or prayer. Be both patient and ready at the same time.
- Pick up this book and let your eyes fall on a topic that engages you or mirrors where you are at the moment. Look over what I wrote about my experience, read the "Reflections" section that elaborates on the encounter, and consider the "Wisdom" that is offered to engage your imagination.
- Notice what memories, questions, and feelings bubble up inside you. Feel your feelings and notice them in your body.
- Express your responses in writing or in your chosen mode. Use one or more of the questions posed in the "For Your Consideration" sections as prompts or, if you prefer, work free form.

- Date the entries to help document your journey. Dementia caregiving can make life a busy blur, and dates help put your experiences into the context of your full life.
- Follow your reflecting with silence, and maybe a prayer.

Patterns of your life may be revealed as you reflect. You may see repetition. If so, that's important. Responses recur until we get to the bottom of our feelings and questions. While some patterns are cherished, others are imprisoning. But patterns can be changed. This is an opportunity for unexpected beginnings.

Part One

Starting the
Long Walk

Chapter One

· · · · · ·

"We Have Dementia"

Believing that life is fair used to be easy for me. It just seemed common sense that we reap what we sow. Tom's dementia disabused me of that. Dementia was not a just reward for a life lived with compassion and integrity.

Tom and I were supposed to be leading spiritual retreats from our home near Laramie, Wyoming, where the mountains would invite us out for frequent visits, the university would offer cultural and intellectual stimulation, and the cathedral would offer solace. There was to be a large round table in the kitchen for conversation and humor shared with guests and friends over home-cooked meals. There was to be lots of space outside with a small chapel, a sweat lodge, and a yurt to house guests. We were going to lead discussions of global issues and weighty matters of justice and spirituality.

Yet here we were instead, silently sitting in the zinnia-filled courtyard in an Indiana care home, Tom in his wheelchair and me on a bench next to him, my journal open and my pen in hand. I had tried to make Tom comfortable, able only to guess how to do that, because he no longer had words. He couldn't express himself with facial gestures, now that his facial muscles were flaccid. I released the back of the wheelchair so he could lie flat, and I put a small pillow under his head, a pillow I made from soft denim fabric that was once part of his well-worn blue jeans.

When I first met him, Tom owned no other clothes than denim jeans, T-shirts, and a fleece-lined jacket, appropriate wear for working outdoors at the retreat center where he and his partners offered hospitality to city slickers like me. The Antelope Retreat Center offered guests a window into rural life—irrigating hay fields, bottle-feeding the bum lambs discarded by the professional shepherds, shopping once a week in the supermarket sixty miles away. The Center had introduced me to Native American spirituality taught by elders from Yankton Reservation in South Dakota. Guests participated in sweat lodge ceremonies, which proved to be profound prayer meetings, and we experienced solo vision quests in the high sun-soaked Red Desert.

The same bright sun was shining on us, but the earth had shifted. His sun-bleached ponytail had been cut off. His blue eyes were no longer sparkling, nor were they focused. The mouth that had easily sung and whistled now hung open. His once powerful upper body was disfigured: the contractions in his neck caused his head to be permanently twisted toward his left shoulder. His legs and arms (and sometimes his torso) shuddered with unpredictable muscular spasms. The myoclonic movements, like mini seizures, were with him constantly except when he was in a deep sleep. Outside in the open air that he loved so much, sleep did come to him as the cicadas chirped their seasonal music and the wind gently ruffled the leaves above us. Before his own diagnosis, Tom, aware of his father's dementia, told me, "If I ever lose my mind, take me to the Red Desert and leave me. Don't come to find me." He got only part of his wish. There was no Wyoming desert in the care home, only the wilderness that dementia created for him.

And I couldn't find him, no matter how hard I tried.

Reflections

Dementia is not an altogether solo experience. Shortly after his diagnosis, Tom said, "I don't have dementia. *We* have dementia." He spoke a truth I only learned as I lived into it. How wise he was!

No dementia is solitary, especially for those whose lives have intertwined. We walk together, caregiver and care recipient, each having a different experience with the same dementia. We walk together even if we are living apart. We walk each other home, even though dementia takes us to different destinations.

During Tom's illness, I intermittently wrote in my journal. I did not want to lose the complicated, multilayered, bittersweet experience of loving him through it all. In reading the entries later, I watched myself going through the ordeal of Tom's moving further and further away from me. I noticed how I responded, amazed at my varied reactions. Some of the responses were quite gratifying. Some, just as strong and frequent, made me feel embarrassed. Some responses seemed antithetical to each other, yet they were all there and all mine.

We are given hints as to how to manage the journey of dementia caregiving, but we have no dependable road map to tell what to expect. We all learn by doing. We are confused amateurs, trailblazing through unchartered territory. At times, we catch a surprise glimpse of the former personality of the one we care for. At times, we find things inside our hearts that we didn't expect and find them quite mysterious. Few other people seem to notice that we "have dementia" too, that we are being changed by it. Our dreams and former expectations are forfeited to the realities of dementia.

The journey, both the inner exploration and the public odyssey, is not one we chose or wanted, but one we were given. We live it, step by step, because there is no alternative route.

Wisdom

Traveler, your footprints
are the only road, nothing else.
Traveler, there is no road;
you make your own path as you walk.
As you walk, you make your own road,
and when you look back
you see the path

you will never travel again.
Traveler, there is no road;
Only a ship's wake on the sea.

—Antonio Machado[1]

The bad news is we don't have any control. The good news is we can't make any mistakes.

—Chuck Palahniuk[2]

Maps only get you to destinations already discovered, but to discover the unknown you need to burn your maps and walk free, unrestrained and unconditioned like the wind.

—Abhijit Naskar[3]

Though your destination is not yet clear
You can trust the promise of this opening;
Unfurl yourself into the grace of beginning
That is at one with your life's desire.

—John O'Donohue[4]

For Your Consideration

- What future had you hoped for in your relationship with the one for whom you care? Let your imagination take you to that dreamed-of place.
- In what ways has dementia changed the relationship you had?
- What changes do you foresee coming? What fears do those anticipated changes bring?
- Is there a compass you look to for navigating through life? Are you finding it dependable on the journey of dementia caregiving?

Chapter Two

• • • • • •

A Look at Caregiver Needs

Getting legal documents in order, finding a suitable and affordable adult day care service, connecting with people who could care for Tom in my absence—all these activities were demanding of my time. They were worth the investment because having such practical issues handled meant I had a semblance of order. This offered some structure, which freed up my mind to seek snippets of "me time." That, however, was hard to find.

When I was frenetic, my friends and my doctor advised me, "Take care of yourself." Easier said than done. I realized that what I really wanted was a quick fix, maybe a pill, to cure my anxiety and fears and magically put more hours into the day. Such a pill doesn't exist, of course, and in truth, if it did, it would have been nothing but a superficial and temporary answer.

Reflections

Our needs as dementia caregivers can be viewed in many ways. I offer two perspectives, different but compatible. One emphasizes the practical needs we face, building from the most basic to the less tangible needs.

The other looks at the way we express our needs, moving from the most obvious expressions to deeper, more subtle levels.

The Pyramid Model

Stephan G. Wiet[1] is a psychologist and researcher who developed the "Caregiver Needs Pyramid," often referenced to as the "Hierarchy of Caregiver Needs." The foundation of the pyramid is the most basic level: needing *help to make better decisions* in legal, medical, and financial areas. These are the first needs we face, and much time and energy are focused here.

After these basic concerns are addressed, the next level of need is *simplifying life* by distinguishing between what is absolutely necessary and what can be let go or delegated. It includes identifying who and what can help with giving care. Many books and websites focus on supporting dementia caregivers with the practical issues of these levels, thank goodness.

Once these needs are given due consideration and the caregiver's life is more simplified, the caregiver can move to the next level of the pyramid and *find some peace* of mind. Stress starts to lessen with the assurance that the loved one's needs are met, even when the primary caregiver is absent.

Atop the pyramid is the need that Wiet says is rarely acknowledged by caregivers: *finding personal time.* Personal time is necessary for caregivers to pay attention to their emotional needs, and Wiet says that over 90 percent of caregivers report they need more help managing their emotions. To arrive at the top of the pyramid is extremely challenging, and too few are able to get there.

The Iceberg Model

This model, developed by John Travis and Regina Sara Ryan, looks like a pyramid, but it's actually an iceberg. It doesn't focus on human needs, but addresses how those needs are expressed through a person's health, often without words.[2]

The tip of the iceberg, rising above the ocean's surface and visible to all, is the caregiver's *overall state of health*. It's the self that others see. The tip of the iceberg may look enormous and may appear to be all there is, but in relation to the submerged whole, the tip is small. In terms of physical health, the signs of a person's state of well-being are measurements like blood pressure or weight. In terms of spiritual health, the signs include the degree of distractibility with which we go about life, or the confidence with which we meet the challenges of the day.

Just below the surface is the *lifestyle/behavioral level*: the habits from which the visible state of health emerges. In terms of physical health, that might be drinking too much, or driving ourselves so hard that blood pressure rises. We have spiritual habits, too, like whether we ever take time to "stop and smell the roses." Sadly, too many of us never developed good habits of taking care of ourselves in body or soul.

Deeper than the habits of lifestyle is the *cultural/psychological/ motivational level*: the things that drive the habits and choices that manifest themselves in our lifestyle and behaviors. It reflects our psychological makeup, the way we see ourselves in the world. At this level, we might explore questions like, "Am I seeking comfort from food when I know that food will never really satisfy what I need most deeply?" In terms of spiritual health, we might ask, "What are the messages I have internalized about the value of independence?" or "What was I taught about guilt?"

The deepest layer is so big that the authors don't even call it a level; they call it a realm: the *spiritual/being/meaning realm*. It's so deep that it can never be fully explored. Here the most significant questions are asked, ones that impact all the layers above, both physically and spiritually: "Am I loved?" and "What, or who, is God, in light of my loved one's losing their precious mind?"

Both models are needed to understand and tell the whole story of our needs as dementia caregivers. We must climb up the pyramid of practicality in order to find some peace of mind and we must burrow down into our own depths to save our own souls. If we never go deeper than the visible level of our state of health, we only skim the top of our lives. We are not fully living our one and only precious life.

Wisdom

It's not the load that breaks you down, it's the way you carry it.

—Lou Holtz[3]

Women never have a half-hour in all their lives (except before or after anybody is up in the house) that they can call their own without fear of offending or hurting someone. Why do people sit up so late, or, more rarely, get up so early? Not because the day is not long enough, but because they have no time in the day to themselves.

—Florence Nightingale, 1820–1910

Sufficiency isn't two steps up from poverty or one step short of abundance. It isn't a measure of barely enough or more than enough. Sufficiency isn't an amount at all. It is an experience, a context we generate, a declaration, a knowing that there is enough, and that we are enough.

—Brené Brown[4]

For Your Consideration

- How are you dealing with the basic decisions that need to be made—the legal and practical issues? Who is helping with those? Who else might help if you were to ask?
- What do people see when they look at you? What do they see as your state of physical and spiritual health? Is this the way you want to be seen?
- What lifelong habits do you bring to caregiving? These are probably habits that both help and hinder your adapting to your new role.
- Can you imagine how it would feel to find time for yourself? What are the positives of having time for yourself? What are the downsides?
- Can you begin to articulate your own needs? Are they needs to improve your caregiving or are they needs to maintain your own health?

Chapter Three

• • • • • •

What It Means to Care

My work at times required travel, and it was our habit that Tom would collect me from the airport when I returned. He would wait as close to the arrival gate as he could without breeching security. Joy always lit his face when our eyes met; even after years of being together, my heart would skip a beat when I saw him again. We would embrace and kiss, oblivious to other arriving passengers. It was never a very long hug, just a hint of what would happen when we got to our home after our candlelight dinner at Rick's Boatyard Restaurant.

One Monday evening, things changed. Tom met me at the airport, but the message of his eyes was different. No longer was it, "I'm so glad you are home!" Instead, his eyes told me, "What a relief! She's back. I'm safe." Imperceptible to others, the subtle change in his facial expression struck me to my core. A week before, I had been his lover; now I was a symbol of security. I left as a wife and returned as a caregiver.

With his diminishing cognitive ability, Tom certainly needed to know where he was safe in the world. It was flattering to know that I could give him the protection he sought. Yet how could I not grieve the shift of the ground upon which I thought I stood? And if I felt this movement, how much more had life shifted for Tom?

My caregiving changed dramatically over time. I cut back my hours at work, taking a substantial cut in pay, which meant less income in the present and a smaller pension in retirement. I rearranged the way I worked, stuffing more work into the time I could be assured of having day care or respite care for Tom, knowing that my time with him was limited and couldn't be postponed. As I made changes to allow more time with him, I learned viscerally what it meant to care.

Reflections

Caring is complicated, yet we use the word as though everyone knows what it means, despite its wide variations, all the way from writing a check for a good cause, to being vigilant of another person, to changing that person's diapers.

So, what is caring?

The Oxford Dictionary defines caring as "the work of looking after those unable to care for themselves." Because caring is private and out of the public eye, it's hard to describe care more definitively, says the late Peta Bowden, who wrote extensively on nursing and ethics. She claims that the invisibility of caring refers to the difficulty in specifying or prescribing the complex of emotional and material concerns that caring entails, the subsequent tendencies to reduce care to its visible objective tasks, and the denial of the value inherent in its complexity.[1]

Joan Tronto,[2] a university professor whose work combines politics and caring, categorizes caring into phases:

- *Caring about* is recognizing that a need exists and deciding that something has to be done about it. The Alzheimer's Association cares about dementia, and in so doing was caring about Tom. It's a somewhat distant kind of caring.
- *Taking care of* happens when someone assumes some responsibility for meeting a need. Tom's son, who lived two thousand miles away, paid for a suitable wheelchair for his six-foot-two, two-hundred-pound father. He was taking care of his dad. Often this

kind of caring is highly regarded in our society, and it is often men who do it.

- *Caregiving* is the direct meeting of the needs for care. Caregivers are in physical contact with the care receiver. It's hands-on work. It's often gendered as women's work and is not well-paid or valued publicly.
- *Care-receiving* occurs when care is accepted by a person. Our society doesn't think highly of those who receive care, often seeing care receivers as weak. They are seen as helpless and therefore pitiable.

Rosalynn Carter[3] famously reminds us that all of us have been cared for and that all of us either are caregivers, will be caregivers, or will be care-receivers. It's unavoidable. Yet our society largely does not value caregiving. Caring is minimalized and marginalized, viewed as a private matter rather than a social responsibility. Those who are paid to give care are not well remunerated. Those who give care but are unpaid (we are called "informal caregivers") do not have our considerable labor recognized as legitimate work by the US government, thus it is not worthy of credit toward Social Security.

Caring is heavily gendered. Women have been socialized to give care; it is deemed "natural" for women. It seems that if something is "natural" (at least for women), it doesn't warrant compensation. Research shows:

- About 66 percent of dementia caregivers are women, caring for a spouse or partner, and giving care at home.
- It is more common for wives to provide informal care for a husband than vice versa.
- On average, female caregivers spend more time giving care than male caregivers.
- Two and a half times as many women as men report living with the person with dementia full time.[4]

Despite its being disparaged, caring is crucial and central to human life, or as social worker Sheila Neysmith says, "Caring is pivotal to keeping the human enterprise going."[5] You and I choose to care. How can we put a dollar sign on love?

Wisdom

In our present culture there is a great ideological advantage to gain from keeping care from coming into focus. By not noticing how pervasive and central care is to human life, those who are in positions of power and privilege can continue to ignore and to degrade the activities of care and those who give care. . . . It's hard [for "self-made" people] to admit the degree to which care has made their lives possible, but such an admission would undermine the legitimacy of the inequitable distribution of power, resources, and privilege of which they are the beneficiaries.

—Joan Tronto[6]

The overcommitted helper appears to eschew all personal comfort and private interest in the name of service to others. The reality, however, is often quite other. The hidden rewards are so great that this seeming selflessness is a form of self-assertion, which seeks to deny the reciprocity in all acts of caring and to keep the helper firmly in the ranks of the strong and the need-free.

—Alistair Campbell[7]

There is a selflessness in caring . . . that includes heightened awareness, greater responsiveness to the other and to myself, and the fuller use of my distinctive powers. . . . When I use things like trust, courage, responsibility, devotion, and honesty, I grow. That brings me closer to the self-actualization I can experience. It's not that I care in order to grow, but that I grow in the process of caring.

—Milton Mayerhoff[8]

For Your Consideration

- How would you define caring? Has your understanding of caring changed in light of your work in dementia caring?
- How does your community value caring? How does that get shown?

- Who else is caring for your loved one? How are they doing it? In what ways does this also offer care to you?
- How does caring fill you up? How does it deplete you? Does caring ever trap you?
- Do you have strong responses to any of the above quotations in the "Wisdom" section? If so, which one? What is your response?

Part Two

Companions

Chapter Four

● ● ● ● ● ●

The One for Whom You Care

Tom and I were "an item" for years. We easily played off each other's energy, learning how to work together and be silly together. What joy we had in honoring and respecting each other's uniqueness!

Dementia, when it came, worked to change that. At first, I overcompensated for Tom's loss of abilities, which irritated him and exasperated me. As his behaviors and moods became more problematic, I found myself embarrassed—like the night he left me and our friends at our dinner table and returned stark naked to say it was time for his shower. Or the symphony concert when he stepped into the aisle, bowing deeply to the orchestra. Or when he whistled his own tune as we sang a hymn in church.

The person with whom I started this journey changed, incrementally at first, into a person whom others found hard to recognize as Tom. What did not change was the fact that I loved him.

Reflections

You and I would never take this arduous journey of long-term caregiving except that we care about someone with dementia. That someone becomes our most intimate traveling companion. We entered the relationship by chance of birth, or by a turn of circumstance, or by our choosing. Our loved one may be a parent, a sibling, a friend, a partner, or a spouse. Though our intimate companions are quite different from each other, what is common is our care for them. Our motivations may vary and our caring may take very different shapes and have different intensities and longevities, but it is care nevertheless.

Traveling companions face the same dementia, live in the same time, hear the same information, and witness the same losses; yet, for all the sameness, the two are having different experiences. In the 1950 Japanese film *Roshoman*, various characters provide subjective, alternative, and contradictory versions of the same incident, leaving the audience to wonder which story is accurate. The truth is that each character has their own experience, rooted in personal, uncontestable conviction. It's the same for the caregiver and the one cared for, as each has a distinct experience.

When two people commit themselves to each other in some way, it's a bit like the ritual that is at times used in wedding ceremonies called the Lighting of the Unity Candle. Each person who is taking vows holds a lit taper and together they light a third candle that represents their new life. A *we* comes into being. Over time, energies blend into a common history and lives entwine by the sharing of mutual daily life. If things are going well—really well—those who made the promises hardly want to claim their original individuality, so happy are they with the *we*.

If things are not going well, or if the *we* that was created is not healthy, a sense of dread sets in along with a diagnosis of dementia. What was at best tolerable prior to the diagnosis becomes full of doom and resentment. This happens when abuse or alcoholism has been part of the shared history, or when there are serious still unresolved conflicts. It can happen when a daughter or a spouse feels a socially imposed obligation to give care. It can happen when there's a sense of past guilt that needs to be atoned, or when there's an old obligation in need of repayment. If both parties were actually able-bodied and the original selves could still grow individually, there might be resolution, possibly to separate from each other or possibly to grow together. But that can't happen after a dementia diagnosis. One partner is prisoner of a diseased brain, and this kind of growth won't be possible.

If this describes your situation, remember that you still have options. Maybe there is a way, with the help of a counselor, to work through some of the difficulty before the dementia becomes full-blown. Maybe ongoing individual counseling can help get you through this despite your companion's illness. Or maybe you will need to remove yourself from the role of caregiver, hard as that might be, knowing that you have good reason—for your own well-being as well as that of the person with dementia.

When dementia sets in, even the healthy *we* starts to change. It is shocking to see something so precious start to dissolve. Some of us try to preserve what had been, trying to take on the life of our loved one in service to their loss of personality. We try to keep the former *we* intact, making excuses for odd behaviors and begging off invitations that might prove awkward.

But our loved ones are other than us. They always were. Although a *we* was created, the individuals who made that *we* were not extinguished; each is having a different experience of dementia. Our loved ones' disinhibitions, or hallucinations, or forgetfulness, or poor judgment are not ours. They do not reflect on us or on our caregiving, and they need not embarrass us. We cannot enter into our loved ones' lives and fix what is broken any more than we can keep the former *we* alive in its former iteration.

Trying to swallow another's life in our own is both audacious and futile. We are made to live our own lives; we are neither qualified nor entitled to live the life of another.

Wisdom

. . . Often I am reminded
that the time may come (for this is our pledge)
when you will stand by me and know

that I, though "living" still, have gone beyond
all remembering, as my father went in time
before me. . . .

But I know now that in the great distance
on the edge or beyond the edge of this world

I will be growing alight with being. And (listen!)
I will be longing to come back.
. . . On time's edge, wakened,
shaken, light and free, I will be longing

to return, to seek you through the world,
to find you (recognizing you by your beauty),
to marry you, to make a place to live. . . .

I see that it is
imperfect. It will be imperfect. (To whom would love
appear but to those in most desperate need?) Yes,

I would err again. Yes, we would suffer
again. Yes, provided you would have it
so, I would do it all again.

—Wendell Berry[1]

Afoot and light-hearted I take to the open road,
Healthy, free, the world before me,
The long brown path before me. . . .
I give you my love more precious than money,
I give you myself . . . .
Will you give me yourself? Will you come travel with me?
Shall we stick by each other as long as we live?

—Walt Whitman[2]

For Your Consideration

- What was the essence of your relationship with your loved one before dementia? Has the essence of your relationship changed? How does this influence your caregiving?

- What things, both big and small, do you miss most about the relationship you had before dementia?
- What did you love in that person in the past? What do you love in that person now?
- Wendell Berry says he "would do it all again." Whatever form your earlier relationship was with the one for whom you care, would you do it all over again? Why is that?
- If your loved one had never been in your life, how would your life have been different?
- What deep values do you hold that can guide you now, as you walk together on this difficult journey?

Chapter Five

• • • • • •

Other Dementia Caregivers

The first support group meeting that Tom and I attended was at our local Alzheimer's Association office, a plain, low building just off a major intersection of highway on a city street. The room was nothing to speak of. But the people!

Two skilled social workers, contracted by the local Alzheimer's Association, met around a long table with twelve couples in the early stage of dementia. We were twenty-four ordinary people, twelve with a new diagnosis and twelve (all women) who were becoming caregivers. We didn't consider ourselves old, just people in our fifties and sixties, one couple in their seventies. It was obvious from our strained faces and our initial silence that we were frightened at the prospect of what lay ahead of us.

We committed to meeting monthly. It felt daring to have frank and honest conversations, the diagnosed and the "healthy" side-by-side. The sessions were informational and practical, giving us the basics of what to expect and how to prepare for this new future. After an hour, we broke into two groups, one for future caregivers and one for future care receivers, each group facilitated by a social worker.

The group morphed over the years. When the Alzheimer's Association chapter no longer had money to pay the facilitators, the social workers volunteered to help us to regroup on our own. We found an adult day care that was willing to let us meet on their premises if we paid an aide to care for the men as their abilities waned. Couples dropped out: The most elderly pair, Sarah and Al, after an attack of shingles severely lowered his ability to function; Jill and Pete, after the heart attack that killed him; Judith and Charles, who felt the intensity of the group's sharing was too much for their introversion.

Ten years later, the twelve couples had become four couples and many singles. We no longer needed the adult day care facility. Three of the surviving men needed twenty-four-hour care and lived apart from their partners. Jim alone had held steady over the years. The women met monthly at a restaurant and shared our lives over a meal. We met at funerals to share each other's grief. We even met after we were widowed, and again at two new marriages. We knew we were not alone.

Reflections

Is this a typical support group? I doubt it. But it did exist, meaning it is possible to have deeply meaningful connections with other caregivers who started out as complete strangers. If we were not in a city, if we did not have transportation, or if the Alzheimer's Association had not had the vision to gather us initially, we would never have met and we would have been poorer for it. There are other ways of getting support, but dementia caregivers meeting face-to-face reassures us that we have companions along the way.

Up-to-date information about our larger cohort of caregivers is available through the annual report of the Alzheimer's Association.[1] The document is a window into what noncaregivers are saying about us. Who are we as a group?

- There are about 11.2 million of us in the United States alone.
- About 40 percent of us have an annual income of $50,000 or less.
- About 25 percent are "sandwich generation" caregivers, people giving care to both children as well as to aging parents.
- We "informal" or "family" caregivers provided an estimated 15.3 billion hours of unpaid care, a contribution to the nation valued at $256.7 billion, or approximately 12 times the total revenue of McDonald's in 2019.

There are concerns unique to dementia caregivers who are still gainfully employed. Of those caregivers who also hold down jobs outside the home:

- 57 percent have been late to work or left early compared with 47 percent of nondementia caregivers.
- 18 percent went from full-time to part-time work.
- 9 percent gave up gainful employment completely, and
- 8 percent turned down promotion.

All the while, dementia caregivers bore nearly twice the average out-of-pocket costs of nondementia caregivers.

Marilyn Geewax wrote for National Public Radio about working women who are caregivers. She reveals:

> The MetLife report said that for the typical woman, the lost wages due to dropping out of the labor force because of adult caregiving responsibilities averages nearly $143,000. That figure reflects the wages lost while not working—typically for about five years—as well as lower wages after returning to the workforce with rusty skills. When foregone pension and Social Security benefits are counted, the out-of-pocket losses roughly double.[2]

Clearly, we are not in this for the money. And we aren't in it because it's easy. We were not educated or certified or licensed for the role of caregiver. We never applied for the job. We weren't even screened. We have no job description to follow, and no supervisor to offer support. We don't get a forty-hour work week with weekends off.

Nor are we in it for the health benefits.[3] We have great stress. Compared with caregivers of people without dementia, twice as many of us have substantial emotional and physical difficulties. Thirty to forty percent of us suffer from depression. Three-quarters of us report being concerned about our own health, and rightly so, considering that as a group we have significant cardiovascular problems, lowered immunity, and increased chronic illness. We take more medications and have less engagement in good health behaviors (exercise, sleep, eating well) than our noncaregiving cohorts.

So why do we do it? What's our motivation? The 2021 Alzheimer's Disease Facts and Figures says the three primary reasons caregivers provide care are (1) the desire to keep a family member or friend at home, (2) proximity to the person with dementia, and (3) the caregiver's perceived obligation to the person with dementia.[4] I can't help but wonder how we are also motivated by the astronomical cost of care outside the home.

Describing motivations for dementia caregiving through a different lens, Suzanne Cahill found we are motivated by five factors: love, obligation, duty, commitment, and guilt.[5] In 1997 researchers found that important questions about motivation have not yet been asked, like, "How do prior values influence the decision to provide care?" and "How is it that people find or create meaning in giving care?"[6] Another quarter century on, researchers are still unclear as to what makes us tick.[7] Clearly, motivation is complicated and influenced by many factors: cultural expectations, whether or not we experience reciprocity in the relationship, whether or not we have a sense of coherence between what we do and what we believe—the list goes on.

For all the differences between caregivers, one thing is quite clear: Our values impact our decision to care, and in turn, our experience of caring impacts our values. For all the differences between us, we are on a common journey, and we are not alone.

Wisdom

Listen! I will be honest with you,
I do not offer the old smooth prizes, but offer rough new prizes,
These are the days that must happen to you:

You shall not heap up what is call'd riches,
You shall scatter with lavish hand all that you earn or achieve. . . .
What beckonings of love you receive, you shall only answer
with passionate kisses of parting. . . .

—Walt Whitman[8]

Care allows creatures to escape our explanations into their actual presence and their essential mystery. In taking care of our fellow creatures, we acknowledge that they are not ours; we acknowledge that they belong to an order and harmony of which we ourselves are parts.

—Wendell Berry[9]

Our attitude toward all . . . would be Christian if we regarded [others] as though they were dying, and determine our relationship with them in light of death, both of their death and our own. A person who is dying calls for a special kind of feeling. Our attitude to [them] is at once softened and lifted onto a higher plane. . . . Every [person] is dying. I too am dying and must never forget about death.

—Nicholas Berdyaev[10]

For Your Consideration

- Can you see yourself joining a support group? Is there something that keeps you from participating in one? What might that be? How might that be addressed?
- In what ways do you match or differ from statistically described dementia caregivers? Can you envision this cohort of caregivers being your true traveling companions?
- What has dementia cost you?
- Suzanne Cahill describes motivations for caregiving as love, obligation, duty, commitment, and guilt. If you make a pie chart of your motivations, what percentage would each occupy?
- Nicholas Berdyaev recalls an ancient monastic practice, *memento mori*, which is an admonition to remember our death. Is remembering your own mortality helpful in your caregiving?

Chapter Six

• • • • • •

Your God

The God of my childhood is not the God I know now, and probably isn't the God I'll know at my death.

As a six-year-old, at a tent meeting during summer camp, I walked forward to the preacher and was saved. My mother was pleased. Back home in Brooklyn, she sent me to the Gospel Mission, a storefront church just a block from our house. They taught me that belief in Jesus is what mattered above all else, that I was born in sin and needed redemption, that Jesus died to atone for my sin, and that each person had to give their heart to Jesus or be damned to hell. That is not the way I understand or experience Christianity today, but leaving my early beliefs took time, thought, prayer, and life experience. It was hard to leave the faith of my mother, for she was earnest and loved me beyond words.

It was hard to leave the certainty of her form of Christianity, inculcated in me so early and deeply. Some people never leave the faith of their fathers or mothers, be that traditional religion, agnosticism, or atheism, and I understand why. Changing one's beliefs is not what everyone feels the need to do. There's wisdom in the adage, "If it isn't broken, don't fix it."

My religion, however, was broken. Seeing the good lives of people of other faiths or no faith caused me to wonder about the convictions of the Christianity I had been taught. God's silence to my pleas made me question the efficacy of the style of prayer to which I had become accustomed.

Witnessing the suffering of innocent people led me to inquire about the nature of a loving God.

I was in my thirties when I first heard from a pulpit the story of Adam and Eve referred to as a myth. I was surprised and much relieved. In my forties, I questioned "original sin" and found that there are alternatives to that theory attributed to Augustine, as there are alternatives to Anselm's "substitutionary atonement" theory, which holds that because God demands justice, Jesus was punished in the place of sinful humans. Richard Rohr says that my early religion creates a mercantile Christianity with God as the major debt collector.[1]

Maybe the medieval theologian John Duns Scotus had it right, that Jesus was not necessary, but a pure gift. Maybe Jesus's life was to model the best way to live—faithful in relating with God, true to deep convictions, fearless in the face of wrong, honest in witnessing suffering, and accepting the consequences of consciously made decisions. And maybe, just maybe, God is known to different people in different ways, all truth being God's truth.

In my fifties, watching Tom's decline, I asked many questions—questions that no one ancient or modern answered to my satisfaction, though it was not for lack of effort. There's much written about theodicy, or "why bad things happen to good people." My questions took me to Rabbi Harold Kushner's classic book. I considered the Buddhist concept of suffering. I read the book of Job and its many commentaries. I questioned a God who was only love when I saw Tom's terrifying hallucinations that neither he nor God nor anyone else could control.

Alongside my questions and doubts, I witnessed a loving God live in those around me—the friends who would bring me supper when I was exhausted, the man from church who committed to taking Tom on a weekly walk through the nearby nature preserve, and the gentle staff of Joy's House, the adult day care that became my professional salvation. And I saw the God of love when Tom crossed over into late-stage dementia and stopped fighting his extreme limitations.

My questions are likely to continue to be part of my faith journey. Honest relationships mature and deepen, and I expect this to be the case in my friendship with God until my own death—and maybe beyond.

Reflections

What does *God* mean? Different things to different people, of course. Popularly speaking, God is a supernatural being worshipped by humans and called by various names like Allah, Jehovah, and Great Spirit. Some people describe such a supernatural being using attributes like almighty, creator, and omnipotent. Other people understand God through use of the *via negativa*, finding it impossible to describe the divine with human attributes or concepts, saying that God can never be encapsulated by words. Agnostics make space for the possibility of a God who is totally unknowable by rational thinking, finding insufficient evidence to justify belief that God does or does not exist. Atheists believe that God does not exist, attributing the good and the bad in the world to nature and putting their trust in the human enterprise.

There will never be a universal understanding of the meaning of *God*, but I think we each come up with some working definition to get us through life. Almost automatically and quite naturally, humans reflect on the existence of a God, and one doesn't need formal religious education to do that. Our understandings may change as we change. For me, that's not waffling; it's maturing.

For purposes of this book, I use the word *God* fully aware that it carries baggage for many. I trust that when you see the word *God* written here, you will read it as the God you know—a Higher Power, the Universe, Spirit, the Other, the Mystery. And if you don't believe in a God, maybe you can see the word as meaning your own "Better Angel."

Rudolf Otto, the early twentieth-century theologian, introduced me to ideas that helped me understand my latest experience of God. He says God is the *mysterium tremendum et fascinans,* and though the vocabulary is probably foreign, the concepts aren't. *Mysterium* refers to the wholly Other, that which is beyond our experience in ordinary life. *Tremendum* is power that is terrifying; it is might that is utterly majestic. *Fascinans* refers to attraction; it is the pull toward grace despite fear and trepidation. Together, these words describe Otto's understanding of what underlies all religion, a God who is numinous. He describes the human experience of God in this way:

It may at times come sweeping like a gentle tide, pervading the mind with a tranquil mood of deepest worship. . . . It has its wild and demonic forms and can sink to an almost grisly horror and shuddering. . . . It may be developed into something beautiful and pure and glorious. It may become the hushed, trembling, and speechless humility of the creature in the presence of—whom or what? In the presence of that which is a Mystery inexpressible and above all creatures.[2]

Seeing God in this complexity, encompassing the attractive and the frightening, is strangely satisfying to me. It reminds me that God is God and I am not. Such a God can do what God does without my permission or wants or whims. In the book of Job, God asks Job, "Where were you when I laid the foundation of the earth? Tell me, if you have understanding" (Job 38:4). The Job story confirms that God is not in the business of rewarding anyone's good behavior with special favors, and that we mortals are not in charge of the universe. Buddhists might call this understanding a form of enlightenment, seeing the world as it is, with no preconditioned grids, filters, or mirrors. Such a God requires that we take the world as it is, with all that life brings, and that we accept that control does not belong to us.

This understanding freed me to start to live more comfortably with the questions. I learned I could hold things that seemed to be contradictory in the same container. It freed me to see God manifest in the ancient Palestinian Jesus *and* in those who daily supported Tom in his dementia, to encounter God in my extreme loneliness *and* in the community of the Eucharist. It let me see God in the world's many religions that seek a right relationship with God and with others. It let me see God in people who live honestly and courageously and do not name a God.

Most profoundly, it let me see that I did not have to understand God in order to have faith, and that my job is to live faithfully, not perfectly, doing my best to love God and love my neighbor as myself. I haven't left Christianity, though those who hold to a more orthodox faith might think so. Jesus is still my companion along the way. His story is larger than mere facts; his story is truth and even poetry. I prefer to experience God in my living rather than to understand God in my head.

Your God probably looks very different from my God, and that is as it should be. The relationship you have with God is your own, whether that means questioning the existence of God, or walking hand in hand with Jesus, or any other image that reflects your relationship. What matters, I believe, is your being lovingly faithful to your growing experience of God and letting that relationship develop deep roots. That is what faith is.

Wisdom

We have had names for you:
the Thunderer, the Almighty
Hunter, Lord of the snowflake
and the sabre-toothed tiger.
One name we have held back
unable to reconcile it
with the mosquito, the tidal-wave,
the black hole into which
time will fall. You have answered
us with the image of yourself
on a hewn tree, suffering
injustice, pardoning it;
pointing as though in either
direction; horrifying us
with the possibility of dislocation.
Ah, love, with your arms out
wide, tell us how much more
they must still be stretched
to embrace a universe drawing
away from us at the speed of light.

—R. S. Thomas[3]

We make his love too narrow
by false limits of our own;
and we magnify his strictness
with a zeal he will not own. . . .

There is grace enough for thousands
of new worlds as great as this:
There is room for fresh creations
In that upper house of bliss.

—Fredrick Faber[4]

[Note: Augustine famously wrote in his *Confessions* that the heart
is restless until it finds its rest in God. Hafiz knew that wisdom too.
In the poem below, "I" is God.]

There is a Beautiful Creature
Living in a hole you have dug.
So at night
I set fruit and grains
And little pots of wine and milk
Beside your soft earthen mounds,
And I often sing.
But still, my dear,
You do not come out.
I have fallen in love with Someone
Who hides inside you.
We should talk about this problem—
Otherwise,
I will never leave you alone.

—Hafiz[5]

Late and starting to rain, it's time to go home.
We've wandered long enough in empty buildings.
I know it's tempting to stay and meet those new people.
I know it's even more sensible
to spend the night here with them,
but I want to go home.

We've seen enough beautiful places with signs on them
Saying "this is God's house."

That's seeing the grain like the ants do,
without the work of harvesting.
Let's leave grazing to the cows and go
where we know what everyone really intends,
where we can walk around without our clothes on.

—Rumi[6]

For Your Consideration

- Have you at times felt a connection with God? What were the circumstances? How did that feel inside? Has that experience informed how you see life? Has it shaped your caregiving?
- Is your God the same as the God you knew when you were young? Is your God the same as when you started the journey of dementia caregiving?
- If you have experienced a change, what God did you leave behind? What God do you honor now?
- If you have not experienced a change, why is that? What is it that you hold precious?
- If you do not have faith in a God, what does that mean to how you live your life? How does that influence you as a caregiver?
- What do you think Rumi means when he talks about walking around without our clothes on? What would it mean to take that stance before your God?

Part Three

Provisions for
the Journey

Chapter Seven

• • • • • •

A Perspective on Prayer

U ntil dementia became part of my life, I thought I knew how to pray. I'd prayed since childhood, kneeling by my bed and saying the prayers my mother taught me. As I grew, my understanding of prayer enlarged: the long pastoral prayers in the Reformed church next to my childhood home, the extemporaneous prayers with the Baptist youth group, and the collects offered at Morning Prayer at the Episcopal church. Later I came to appreciate that words weren't even necessary for prayer. Intentional action could also be praying, like planting a garden, caring for patients in the hospital, and walking quietly in wild places. Prayer was, as John Montgomery's old hymn says, "the soul's sincere desire, uttered or unexpressed."[1]

Dementia shook up my understanding of prayer as it seems to shake up everything. I felt foolish praying for Tom to be miraculously healed of his illness, calling upon the Creator of the Universe to change the rules and make Tom the exception—the first person ever cured of Alzheimer's. It seemed ludicrous. I was faced with the uncomfortable truth that despite my prayers, God did not particularly protect those who were faithful. God did not shield the helpless. Why was I pretending that prayer "worked"? I knew I needed a different kind of praying, for prayer requires honesty if it requires anything. I had to pass on the magic. My God had to get bigger.

Jeff, a friend of Tom's, taught me a new way to pray. He visited Tom at the care home even when very few others did. Most people were uneasy visiting Tom because they were still caught in the desire to do something, rather than just be someone. But Jeff was different. Unselfconscious and authentic, he was a beautiful blend of Episcopal priest and Quaker spirituality.

Jeff sat with Tom. That's it. He just sat. Neither of them said anything. Tom might whistle, and certainly his limbs would jerk, but there was no observable communication and no repetition of familiar prayers. There was no laundry list to test God as present or not, potent or not. But there was prayer. Jeff was responding to the God he knew as Light and saw Tom in the glow of that Light. Jeff was praying with Tom.

Reflections

How you understand prayer determines whether or not you even choose to read this chapter. If prayer is another thing to add to your already too busy life, you won't be interested; it will sound like more work, more duty. But if you see prayer as a way of being connected with God, you might find a kernel of truth here.

There are many ways to answer the question, "What is prayer?" Some say prayer is a set of words offered to God. Others say it's an earnest hope or a serious request or a joyful thanksgiving addressed to God. One less traditional and more comprehensive definition comes from Ralph Martin, who says, "Prayer is, at root, simply paying attention to God."[2] The *Book of Common Prayer* takes it a bit further, saying, "Prayer is responding to God, by thought and by deeds, with or without words."[3]

There's a word in the Christian Testament of the Bible that is translated "to make intercession"—*entunchanein*. It does not mean making petitions or saying any words at all. It means "to be with someone on behalf of another." Jeff was with God on behalf of Tom. I learned that I was praying when I was next to Tom, letting him know he was not alone. I would seek to open myself to what might be happening inside him.

Sometimes I sensed him to be having hallucinations as his eyes reached around the room, glaring anxiously but focusing on nothing. Sometimes I sensed sadness, and sometimes resigned acceptance. I would take what I sensed in him into my quietness, the place in my heart where I hoped I could meet God. I was being with God on Tom's behalf. Such praying is truly being "in the now," as Tom was in the now. It wasn't remembering, and it wasn't looking to a future. It was simply being in the present, the only place that God can really meet us.

Prayer is not just for people who follow an organized system of beliefs. Religion clearly helps some people, but it has harmed others. Religious or not, each of us has a spiritual self, a divine spark. Our bodies are infused with spirit, and our spirits are infused with body. The mystic and paleontologist Pierre Teilhard de Chardin is said to have claimed boldly, "We are not human beings on a spiritual journey. We are spiritual beings on a human journey."[4]

Spiritual practices help people pay attention to God, as they are tools to help us respond to God in our daily lives. The next chapter describes some of those practices, but for now suffice it to say that prayer is the basic foundation for connecting with God.

Wisdom

Eternal Spirit of the living Christ,
I know not how to ask or what to say;
I only know my need, as deep as life,
and only you can teach me how to pray.

—Frank von Christierson[5]

Prayer is like watching for the Kingfisher.
All you can do is be where he is likely to appear, and Wait.
Often, nothing much happens;
There is space, silence and Expectancy.
No visible sign, only the knowledge that he's been there and may
come again.
Seeing or not seeing cease to matter.

You have been prepared.
But sometimes, when you've almost stopped expecting it,
A flash of brightness gives encouragement.

—Ann Lewin[6]

A piece of iron when kept for long in fire begins not only to look like fire but also to burn like fire. The soul of man in prayer soaks the substance of his being in the divine ocean of light and grace and draws nourishment from it.

—Rumi[7]

For Your Consideration

- Is there anything in the "Wisdom" section that speaks to you, affirming or challenging your understanding of prayer? What does it say to you? How do you respond?
- What do you understand prayer to be? Do any of the definitions suggested in this chapter resonate with you?
- Do you pray? Why or why not?
- If you pray, what motivates you to pray? How does it feel inside when you pray? How do you go about praying? Do you have particular practices?
- What gets in the way of your praying?
- Has dementia caregiving changed your praying? If so, how?

Chapter Eight

• • • • • •

Spiritual Practices

lthough you may not be familiar with the term *spiritual prac-tices*, you probably engage in them unawares. Spiritual practices include but are not limited to saying prayers and reading holy writ, and they are not one more thing to add to the "To Do" list. For one person, gardening is a spiritual practice, as they watch the cycles of life and death and then new life unfold. For someone else, it is attentively watching a film for its message about life's meaning. If you have been journaling, you have engaged in a spiritual practice. Spiritual practices help slow us down, even if it's just for a short while, and help us notice what's going on behind the daily round of busy life. They help us gain a glimpse of God.

Describing the myriad of spiritual practices in a chapter would be impossible. Instead, I have selected a few practices that might fit into the extremely full and often overcommitted lives of dementia caregivers. To see the full breadth of spiritual practices, I encourage you to explore Spirituality and Practice, the online work of Mary Ann and Fredric Brussat.[1]

At Home

Beauty

Beauty is everywhere, if you take the time to notice. I have a series of photographs of rust and peeling paint done by a young artist in Japan. Instead of seeing surfaces in need of fixing, she saw what was actually there—shapes, colors, textures, and the play of light. Beauty can take us beyond the immediate to a deeper message and it can feed our souls. A picture on a wall or a flower in a vase will do—it doesn't have to be much. Removing unnecessary visual clutter can itself reveal beauty and serenity. For other people, visual busyness is comforting. We're all different, and beauty is indeed in the eye of the beholder. Beauty has to be easy on your eyes, only yours. It will take you out of the ordinary to the extraordinary.

Music

Music can open up your spirit. Different kinds of music speak to various elements inside you, and your choice of music can vary as your needs change. Music can comfort, especially old favorites that remind you of kinder times. Your loved one just might relate to this music too, with recognition that surprises you. Music that is wordless, soft, or repetitious can be calming. Music with a strong beat can energize. Music can work subliminally as background sound, and at other times you can concentrate and focus on the music alone. Either way, it can transport you beyond the immediate physical world and connect you with something greater.

Nature

Getting outside to look at nature doesn't mean you have to find a manicured garden or a grand vista; it can be a cloud or persistent dandelion in a crack in the sidewalk. Watch and let it teach. The early Celtic Christians believed a person had to read both the Book of Scripture and the Book of Nature. Nature can be a dynamic partner in growth. It is truly "other" and outside our personal control. Maybe you can make a practice of watching the sun set or rise, seeing that liminal part of the day subtly change. Observing nature requires no expenditure of energy or money, and it opens us to awe.

While Giving Care

Body Scan

You can do this practice right in the middle of caring for your loved one. Take a breath and pay real attention to that breath. Notice the breaths that follow. Are you holding your breath? Are your breaths shallow? Notice what's happening in your body, from your scalp to your toes and everything in between. Where is the tightness? Where is there imbalance? Consciously breathe into that part of your body and let the tightness relax. Your body speaks your mind. It doesn't lie and has much to tell you about your spirit. Listening to your body can be a way of listening to God.

Play

It's okay to find the funny parts in dementia caregiving. God has a sense of humor. Maybe we all could benefit from not taking ourselves so seriously. Play nourishes the soul and builds perspective. Norman Cousins taught us that laughter is very good medicine. Some situations are just so ridiculous that you have to laugh. Watching short silly or even slapstick shows on television might make you laugh. Watching toddlers (for whom you are not responsible) can make smiles. Lightening up releases endorphins, and that's always good! It softens us and keeps rigidity at bay.

Mindfulness

Pay attention, careful attention, to what's right in front of you. It sounds so easy, but we constantly want to move ahead mentally to the next task or revisit thoughts about yesterday. But stay in the moment and engage your senses of smell, sight, hearing, touch. Break down what you are doing into parts. You are not "cleaning him up again"; you are noticing what is happening in the moment. You sense "The wash cloth is warm on my hands. . . . The soap smells like lemon. . . . The urine on his pants makes the color go from khaki to cinnamon. . . ." Yes, it's a mind game, but it focuses your mind, and that in itself helps you relax. Spiritual wisdom would have us live in the now, and I repeat: I firmly believe that here and now is the only place and time we can meet God.

When Alone

Lectio

Lectio simply means reading. Often it is intense reading of a short scriptural text (*lectio divina*), but it could be reading poetry. Read a selected passage aloud. Then pause and recall if some word or phrase stands out. Savor the insight, feeling, or understanding. Pause. Then read the passage again, because it will likely have a fuller meaning. Pause again and note your latest response. This kind of reflective listening allows for a deepened awareness of God speaking to you.

Meditation

Meditation is a mind-clearing, letting your consciousness go from superficial chatter to your deep inner core. It takes much practice to glean the full benefit of meditation, but even an infrequent use of this practice can be enriching. It's like allowing your mind to board an elevator and going down, one floor at a time, till you get to bedrock silence in your soul. If distractions intrude, imagine placing them on a barge that's floating down a river and watching them effortlessly leave your awareness. If your mind wanders, you can bring yourself back to your inner silence with a word (a *mantra*) that grounds you. The word could be religious, like Allah (the One to whom you submit), but it doesn't have to be religious. A *mantra* is a way to anchor yourself in the quiet of the moment. When time is up, possibly signaled by a timer, you can get on the elevator again and slowly return to your everyday consciousness.

Sabbath

This ancient spiritual practice comes from the Jewish tradition of committing one day a week to refrain from impacting Creation in any way and letting the world be what it is. Our society doesn't know Sabbath rest, and alas many of us can't even find five minutes in the day that are not committed to doing something. It doesn't have to be a certain day each week. It could be two hours one afternoon a week that you keep empty, when you haven't planned anything—not even something you enjoy. You arrive at that time and decide then what your heart is asking of you. A nap? A solo walk? Knitting? If you are able to get alternative care for your loved one, maybe you could plan for one completely free day a month. My advice is to put the Sabbath time in your calendar and keep that appointment. It won't happen without your clear intention; no one will do it for you. Remember that the God of Genesis rested. We do well to follow that divine example.

With Others

Hospitality

If it's hard to go out socially due to your loved one's disconcerting behaviors, consider inviting people into your home. You aren't inviting them to a fancy meal or a spotless house, and there is no restaurant etiquette to observe. All you need is a pot of coffee or tea and a few mugs. There's no agenda. Conversation could just be about the weather. The purpose is connecting to the web of life, even when your life is constrained by intense dementia caregiving. God has a way of showing up in other people.

Sharing

Sharing your experience can actually lessen your burden. A support group does that. Your local Alzheimer's Association can tell you where to find such a gathering. If none is available nearby, you might start one. A healthy group allows each participant the space and time to share what's going on inside without judgment. There may or may not be an invitation to respond to what participants say. Giving advice may or may not be part of the sharing. Either way, it's a chance to speak aloud the truth about your current life and to be heard by empathetic others as well as hearing yourself. Sharing reminds you that you are not alone and are part of something bigger.

Spiritual Companionship

Finding a spiritual companion (also known as a spiritual director) allows you to be present one-on-one with someone who is skilled in giving you undivided attention, encouraging you to speak about your life, reflecting back to you what they hear, and posing questions to go deeper to help you find where you are encountering God in your experience. It's not counseling. There's no medical diagnosis. There's no third-party payment. The cost could be anywhere from free on upwards, and many spiritual directors have a sliding scale.[2]

Wisdom

Beauty allows us to forget the pain and dwell on the joy.
                                        —Matthew Fox[3]

Beautiful music is the art . . . that can calm the agitations of the soul; it is one of the most magnificent and delightful presents God has given us.
                                    —Martin Luther (1483–1546)

Every creature is a word of God. If I spent enough time with the tiniest creature—even a caterpillar—I would never have to prepare a sermon. So full of God is every creature.
                            —Meister Eckhart (ca. 1260–1327/28?)

God is the breath inside your breath.
                                        —Kabir (1440–1518)

It takes three things to attain a sense of significant being: God, a soul, and a moment. And the three are always here.

—Abraham Joshua Herschel[4]

For Your Consideration

- Do you currently engage in any of these spiritual practices? How did you choose them—or did they choose you?
- What actions or behaviors make you feel "filled up" inside? What actions bring you a feeling of contentment?
- What moments bring you to a sense of awe?
- Consider becoming engaged more consciously in a spiritual practice. Which practice appeals to you, given your personality and commitments? What might you hope to happen as a result?

Chapter Nine

• • • • • •

Conflicting Encounters

F ortunate to be able to visit a college friend who had moved to Oxford, England, I spent one rainy afternoon walking through the Picture Gallery of Christ Church. I wandered into the early Renaissance collection, and high on the wall was a painting that intrigued me. The subject wasn't unusual—the Virgin Mary sitting with the young Jesus on her lap, the usual suspects in attendance: angels playing musical instruments and saints with faces full of adoration. But something that I found unusual surrounded the Madonna and her son.

The artist had enclosed the figures of Mary and Jesus with an ellipse. I wondered if it might be a medieval aura. Looking more closely, I saw that the ellipse was formed by a chain of objects that looked for all the world like little blue and red zeppelins. Each object had a human face, and with some imagination, I made out wings under each head. Was it a string of angels? Why were they surrounding the holy pair?

The sign below read: "The Virgin with the Child Holding a Rose, in a *Mandorla* of Winged Cherubs' Heads, with Six Saints and Two Musical Angels Below." Mariotto di Nardo or one of his students painted this on wood some six hundred years ago in Florence, Italy. "Ah!" I thought, "so they were angels!" Not the chubby sort I was accustomed to seeing in gift shops, but sleek figures that were on a mission, flying around Mary and

50

Jesus, maybe even protecting them. I was persuaded to explore what the *mandorla* signified.

Mandorla, which means "almond" in Italian, is an ancient symbol that is created when two circles come together and partially overlap. The circles don't merge into one. They remain full circles while allowing something new to be created where they overlap—an almond-shaped space. Medieval artists demonstrated holiness by using the *mandorla* when two different and almost opposing entities—the heavenly and the earthly—come together. Theologically speaking, this is the incarnation, the creation of the God-Man through the mortal woman, who is the Mother of God. Something new and sacred is born.

Reflections

How does all this apply to dementia caregivers? We caregivers live with feelings that are at times in opposition to each other. Paradox can be a daily companion. We feel virtuous and we feel guilty. We feel accepting of the dementia *and* we feel angry at its presence. We know our labor is useful *and* we feel useless to change the course of events. We both question God *and* look to God for comfort.

I have asked other dementia caregivers about their experience. Several said they were telling me things they had not shared before: sexual fantasies that were inconsistent with their beliefs regarding marriage, how unsafe it felt to share their resentments with their noncaregiving friends who imagined caregiving to be pure altruism, the satisfaction they received from caring that was incomprehensible to noncaregivers, and the guilt they felt for wanting to live their own lives apart from the role of caregiver.

The *mandorla* speaks to and critiques the "either/or" mindset of our society that seeks to deem things as either good or bad, right or wrong, beautiful or ugly. The *mandorla* is a symbol of a "both/and" way of thinking. Of course, there are places where we need "either/or" thinking—like which side of the street to drive on—but that's not helpful when it comes to feelings.

Feelings aren't "wrong." They just are. Nice or not, feelings are simply normal. When challenged to choose one feeling over another, we tend to automatically choose the more attractive, socially approved one. We want to look good. We consciously or unconsciously deny the less lovely or inconvenient feeling. The unattended feelings become dangerous— not because society labels them as such but because when they are hidden, they gain power. They invariably come back to bite us when we least expect it. They won't stay hidden.

How can this "both/and" approach work in relation to our contrary feelings? First, we need to decide to allow these opposites to meet each other. The biblical prophet Amos asked, "Can two walk together, unless they be agreed?" (3:3, KJV). Once I would have disagreed, understanding the message to be, "Stay with those who think the way you do." More accurate translations of this verse read, "Do two walk together unless they have agreed to do so?" (NIV) and "unless they have made an appointment?" (NRSV). Two can walk together if they don't see eye-to-eye. They can exchange ideas, listen, allow silence, and permit challenge. The agreement is to get together and interact, not an occasion to find a winner and a loser. New things will happen once the contradictory feelings have faced each other. Each feeling needs to be explored. The truth of each needs to come to the fore. More questions need to be asked: Where are the roots of this feeling? In what ways is it blind or narrow? In what way does it actually apply to the present reality?

Then dialogue between the two can begin. For example, what might the strength of anger have to say to the gentleness of acceptance? Anger brings energy and power. It's forceful and is sometimes overconfident. Its roots probably started growing long before the current situation arose. What about acceptance, this ability to accept what is real though unpleasant? Acceptance has likely been practiced before, and been beneficial. Acceptance brings a peacefulness that is not passivity. Anger and acceptance have much to say to each other.

Dialogue takes place best in the context of prayer, of loving attentiveness to God. As the ancient prayer says, "In quietness and in confidence shall be our strength."[1] Prayer holds open the empty space between the opposites. Just as the hard, durable shell of the almond protects the precious new seed-life inside, so the figurative *mandorla* holds the new and holy place. It can be difficult to penetrate the shell, but it is the only way to get to the fruit.

Holding opposites as both being true is something people of faith have done for centuries. Yehuda Amichai, the Israeli sage, tells us, "A man needs to love and to hate at the same moment, to laugh and to cry with the same eyes."[2] The difficult feelings don't need to be fixed or corrected; they need to be heard. They don't need to be isolated or quarantined from other more pleasant feelings in hope of avoiding infection or conflict. They need to meet the other feelings, overlap, and create an ellipse of holy and mysterious space. It's the place where growth happens.

Wisdom

Whenever you have a clash of opposites in your being and neither will give way to the other . . . , you can be certain that God is present. We dislike the experience intensely and avoid it at any cost; but if we can endure it, the conflict-without-resolution is a direct experience of God.

—Robert J. Johnson[3]

Though we cannot think alike, may we not love alike? May we not be of one heart, though we are not of one opinion? Without all doubt, we may. . . . "If it be, give me your hand." I do not mean, "Be of my opinion." You need not: I do not expect or desire it. Neither do I mean, "I will be of your opinion." I cannot. . . . Keep your opinion and I will keep mine, and that as steadily as ever. . . . Leave all opinions alone on one side and the other: only "give me your hand."

—John Wesley[4]

This being human is a guest house.
Every morning is a new arrival.

A joy, a depression, a meanness,
some momentary awareness comes
as an unexpected visitor.

Welcome and entertain them all!
Even if they're a crowd of sorrows
who violently sweep your house empty of furniture,
still treat each guest honorably.
He may be clearing you out
for some new delight.

The dark thought, the shame, the malice
meet them at the door laughing
and invite them in.

Be grateful for whoever comes
because each has been sent
as a guide from beyond.

—Rumi[5]

The many contradictions in our lives—such as being home but feeling homeless, being busy while being bored . . . can frustrate, irritate, and even discourage us. . . . Yet there is another response. The same contradictions can bring us into touch with a deeper longing for the fulfilment of a desire that lives beneath all desires and that only God can satisfy. Contradictions thus understood, create the friction that can help us move toward God.

—Henri Nouwen[6]

For Your Consideration

- Identify some sets of feelings that are seemingly contradictory to each other. Is there one in the set that you wish would go away? Is it possible to honor that feeling? What benefit does that feeling bring with it?

- How do you answer the prophet Amos's question: "Can two walk together unless they be agreed?" What do you tend to expect when two who don't agree get together? Are there other possibilities?

- Which of your feelings about dementia caregiving are most difficult for you to acknowledge? Why do you suppose that is? Ask these feelings what they have to teach you.

- Do you hesitate to bring differing feelings into conversation with each other? What might be behind that?

Part Four

Encounters along
the Way

Chapter Ten

. . . . . .

Acceptance

To accept that Tom had dementia felt like betraying him. Some symptoms had been there, but there were also alternative explanations. I reasoned he could have attention deficit disorder because wasn't Tom's trouble concentrating and organizing just like people with ADHD? Maybe his behavior was caused by one of those treatable diseases—a poorly functioning thyroid, a benign brain tumor that could be treated with radiation, a clogged carotid artery that could be routed out. I held on to that hope until the cord frayed.

Reality came in the Neurology Clinic. All Tom's test results were finally in—the history and physical, the blood work, the MRI, and the psychometrist's screening. The doctor was a highly respected researcher who was Tom's age and who shared similar interests. Our earlier visits with him had included sharing tales of hiking and camping. But this office visit was different from its start.

The neurologist didn't look at Tom; he looked only at me. The grim pronouncement was made: Tom had mild cognitive impairment, prodromal to Alzheimer's. In plain English, Tom was in the first phase of an illness that would put him out of his mind before killing him. This was the same Tom who, just minutes before, was sitting in the waiting room, calmly leafing through magazines. Our entire world changed in less than five minutes.

I started my resistance to the diagnosis immediately. When the doctor asked me a question, I broke his gaze and looked at Tom, who was still sitting on the patient's table. I asked Tom how he'd answer the doctor's question. The doctor would give me some information, and I would look to Tom and ask what he thought. We were a triangle of people, each with our own agenda and ability to engage, dancing around the news that this was an ailment with no cure.

My profound discomfort raised up the nurse inside me who asked clinical questions to fill the heavy empty space. Even as I spoke, I wondered if the doctor's decision to look only at me and not at Tom was his means of self-protection. Was this good doctor refusing to accept that this strapping, adventurous, fifty-five-year-old man who, like him, loved wilderness, was now a patient he could not mend?

We left with prescriptions and a next appointment, this time for the Alzheimer's Clinic. We drove away from the hospital in silence. Once safely home, still without words, we wept. Then we sobbed. Life would never be the same. There was no way left to deny the diagnosis. But did we have to accept it?

Resistance to this medical information built in me over the next weeks. With me as nurse and pastor, and Tom as a strong mountain man, we could keep the beast at bay, couldn't we? Someone had to be the first person cured of Alzheimer's. Why not Tom? I'd find some research studies in which Tom could participate. Surely someone was on to something in that vast network of laboratories and universities. Weren't there books out there, written by physicians, who promised cures?

Reflections

For a time, resistance—that most useful coping mechanism—serves dementia caregivers well. It's a means of shielding ourselves, keeping away the unwelcomed truths we are not ready to receive. Maybe we resist because we imagine we can keep the good times rolling by sheer dint of will. Maybe we feel that we are betraying our cherished relationship if we let it change. Whatever the motive, it's natural enough to resist the harsh reality initially. Acceptance is the place where we end up, but it is never the place where we start.

At some point, we realize that saying "no" won't make dementia go away. Resistance can't stop the relentless blitz of tangled cells and cotton wool deposits in a beloved brain. Pseudo-acceptance comes first, from the head, providing armor to protect a frightened heart. Real acceptance comes slowly, in tiny doses, and only as we can tolerate it. Acceptance can't and won't be forced or hurried, and there are many "yes, buts" along the way.

An intermediate step between resistance and acceptance might be resignation, where we just allow a thing to be. Resignation is passive, even defeatist. Resignation has no energy. It can keep us stagnant. But on the other hand, it can be a stepping stone to acceptance.

Acceptance requires attention. We begin to accept slowly, from the inside out, not the other way around. We find our own ways of accommodating new truths that are congruent with our love for the one bearing the diagnosis, with the tenderness we need to have for ourselves, and with the natural process of the disease. The essence of love doesn't change, but neither does the essential disease.

Part of acceptance is submission, a "dirty word" to most Western minds. We have been groomed to value our independence and autonomy; we rail at the notion of not being in control. But submission isn't a bad thing. We have all submitted to something, at some time—maybe to the relentless demands of a newborn, maybe to a career that involves humiliating blows in residency or apprenticeship, or maybe to the grueling hours in the law office in order to make partner. Now it's our turn to submit again, this time to a new master. We would do well to learn from Islam. A Muslim is one who submits to God. We can submit consciously and intentionally or submit while kicking and screaming. The difference between resistance and acceptance is the difference between swimming upstream against the current of a mighty river and floating downstream with the river's natural and determined flow.

Eventually, the past has to be just that, the past, the way things were but are no longer. Reality is in the now, not the wished-for future or the remembered past. Facing into reality, though often exceedingly painful, is all that can free us to live and love honestly in the moment. The thirteenth-century mystic Meister Eckhart is credited as saying "There exists only the present instant . . . a Now which always and without end is itself new. There is no yesterday nor any tomorrow, but only Now, as it was a thousand years ago and as it will be a thousand years hence."[1]

Acceptance doesn't mean that we like the hard reality we encounter. These losses are not what we want, but we don't get what we want; we get what we get, and that is all we have to work with. It is only when we are completely defenseless, having laid down our weapons of resistance and denial, that we can truly accept that our loved one is chronically and terminally ill and that, all the while, we can still love them.

When acceptance does come, there is an odd freedom. Energy can be redirected away from a losing battle and toward more important purposes. The gnawing and false sense of responsibility to change the course of the illness is dissipated. We are free to live in the now, choosing to live each day as it is presented, and not struggling to live into a future that could never be. We are free to be ourselves and we free our loved ones to be themselves, showing the world what dementia and loving dementia caring look like.

Wisdom

Do you really think God needs your advice on how to run the world? If this is how things are, it's how they are meant to be; the proof is that if they were meant to be different, they would be.

—Joseph Stein[2]

Freedom is found in limitation. The hand you've been dealt in life has real limitations. . . . Don't invest your life glaring over the fence, either envious or resentful of your neighbors. Long before you poison them, you will poison yourself. Accept the life you've been given. Go and grow from there.

—Curtis Almquist[3]

Holiness is made of dailyness of living life as it comes to us, not as
I insist it be. . . . If we resist, we become the resistance itself.

—Joan Chittister[4]

As we gradually come to befriend our own reality, to look with
compassion at our own sorrows and joys, and as we are able to
discover the unique potential of our way of being in the world, we
can move beyond our protest, put the cup of our life to our lips
and drink it, slowly, carefully, but fully. . . . Drinking our cup is
not simply adapting ourselves to a bad situation and trying to use it
as well as we can. Drinking our cup is a hopeful, courageous, and
self-confident way of living. It is standing in the world with head
erect, solidly rooted in the knowledge of who we are, facing reality
that surrounds us, and responding to it from our hearts.

—Henri Nouwen[5]

For Your Consideration

- For you, what are some of the positive aspects of resistance?
  What are some of the negative aspects?
- How does (or did) it feel to fight the diagnosis? How does (or
  could) acceptance of the diagnosis make you feel?
- Has denial ever imprisoned you or stolen your energies? How so?
- What does submission mean to you? Can you imagine freedom
  in submission?
- On a continuum of resistance-resignation-acceptance, where
  would you place yourself now? Has that changed over time?
- How do you know, or how will you know, that acceptance has
  come?
- Can you imagine ever going beyond acceptance to actually
  embracing dementia caregiving?

Chapter Eleven

• • • • • •

Anger

How much anger can a nice Christian girl have? For a long time, my answer was, "None." The response came from the religion of my youth that taught me a simple way to assure that the sun wouldn't set on my anger was to have no anger. I simply didn't acknowledge my anger. Never mind that Jesus got angry and overturned tables. Never mind that I learned to be passive-aggressive. Somehow, that wasn't "real" anger.

Tom's dementia brought me to the truth about myself. Acknowledged or not, I was very angry. It wasn't constant venom. Rather, it was an ever-present churning just below the surface, willing to erupt at any provocation.

My anger verged on bitterness about what I saw happening to Tom's mind and to our future. I was exasperated cleaning up after Tom urinated again in the corner of the bedroom. I was annoyed that our friends sought us out less often. I was aggravated that the health insurance company couldn't comprehend that Medicare was a secondary, not a primary, insurance. I was indignant that Tom's care at the care home was not above excellent every single minute of every day. I was incredulous that the geriatric-psychiatric unit in the hospital had floor tiles in different colors that, to a brain with dementia, looked like chasms that could be fallen into. I found it incomprehensible that this unit of the hospital was situated above the emergency room with its all-night flashing lights and sirens. On it went, all the way from impatience to fury and back again.

Reflections

Anger is a state of arousal wherein the mind is focused on a potential threat and the body gets ready either to run from it or fight it. Adrenaline and other stress hormones race around the body, the heart rate and blood pressure rise, blood is diverted from the internal organs to the muscles, and the whole self prepares for action. Anger shows in classic facial expressions that are hard to hide. Thinking becomes more primitive and higher intelligence (the part that makes us human) stops working. Anger is a primal, energized state, similar in many ways to sexual arousal, and it can be quite addictive.

When we are really angry, we say we "see red." In order to literally see red through our physical bodies, we need the use of specialized cone cells in the eye. These cells only work when there is some light; when it's dark, the cone cells are useless and we can't see color. Figuratively speaking, maybe we should be thankful that in our anger we "see red" because it means there is some light shed on what's in front of us. We can see what's really happening and do something about it. Anger can be helpful.

Often we conclude that someone else has caused us to be angry. It's tempting to view most human interaction as cause and effect. Although another person's words, or our own memories or fears, may trigger something in us, they do not cause our anger. The feeling is ours, and we need to own our feelings, accept responsibility, and concede that even anger comes from within ourselves. It's an inside job.

When someone or some situation does not meet our expectations, we respond to the difference between "life as we want it to be" and "life as it is" with some degree of anger. We expect people to care for our loved ones the way we would; when they don't, we are angry. We expect people to use "common sense" (meaning the logic we would use); when they don't, we are angry. The amount of anger we feel correlates to the degree of discrepancy between what we expect and what is actual.

Anger, whether it is denied or expressed, rarely stands alone. Social psychologist Carol Tarvis says, "Our emotions are not especially distinctive. They tend to come in bunches like grapes, and it is very rare to find a single emotion causing trouble on its own."[1] Anger can be attached to guilt or blame or fear or sorrow. We don't always think that through. Sometimes it's just easier to get mad than get sad.

Instead of seeing anger as an authentic feeling, we tend to see it as a negative feeling, subscribing to the Gospel of Niceness. Anger at God seems to be the ultimate taboo. Yet in the Holy Scriptures of Jews and Christians, God gets angry. The patriarchs and matriarchs got angry. So famously did the prophets. The seventeenth-century Welsh-born priest-poet George Herbert addressed God as, "Ah, my dear angry Lord."[2] There's a real honesty in anger, even anger at God. God can take it. Our feelings of anger will not make God retaliate or disappear.

Anger, like other feelings, has a message. It is dangerous when acted out in violence or when it is displaced onto someone or something else, but when anger's energy is recognized and harnessed, it has potential to facilitate much good and growth. Feelings are like the spark plugs in old cars. You might look at them, decide you don't like one, and pull it out—but then the car won't work. It needs all the spark plugs, even if they aren't pretty. We need all our feelings to work if we are to be healthy human beings. We need anger. It's a legitimate expression of the human spirit.

How can we handle anger well? Thich Nhat Hahn, presenting a Buddhist approach, encourages us to take compassionate care of our anger. He suggests we treat it as our own little baby needing the attention of being held and rocked. He comments that we wouldn't think of trying to remove our lungs or our heart if they give us trouble, so why would we try to remove anger? Anger is there for a reason. It does an important job. But it needs tending, not to fan the fires but to discover the suffering that is behind it.[3]

C. FitzSimons Allison tells us there are two extremes that we tend to think are the only ways to handle anger. One is to "let off steam," expressing it full throttle. The other is antipodal, to "bottle it up for God" (something that I certainly learned doesn't work).[4] There are many other constructive options for handling anger, with lots of space for subtlety and incremental movement. They all start with our staying with our anger long enough to take responsibility for the feeling and to find its value. Alistair Campbell in *The Gospel of Anger* says that if we "lose anger, love loses its power."[5] If we can't show indignation, we can't show love either.

Finding a safe way to express your anger is a good first step. Anger can be ritualized. I've been known to hit a pillow against my bed, to close the car windows and shout at the top of my lungs, to throw eggs at a tree, and to draw an extreme and ridiculous caricature of the one I was angry with. After safe expression, we can look more deeply into the nature of our anger to see how it has come about: teasing out the root of our anger, seeing how the current situation triggered it, and using reason to take action to fix the presenting problem. Neither globalizing the anger (being angry at everything and everyone) nor catastrophizing the situation (seeing the worst possible outcome) helps. We need to stay specific to the issue at hand, notice what needs to be accomplished and what can get that done. All this may feel a bit inauthentic, especially at first, but all learning is at some level inauthentic until it becomes natural. Remember that by taking good care of ourselves and our anger, we are taking good care of our loved ones too.

Wisdom

Civilized society has an awesome need to cover anger with pleasantness. . . . We carry . . . a load of smiled-over anger, ready to be dumped on any convenient object.

—C. FitzSimons Allison[6]

. . . [T]here sits our sulky sullen dame,
Gathering her brows like gathering storm,
Nursing her wrath to keep it warm.

—Robert Burns[7]

Anger in its time and place
May assume a kind of grace.
It must have some reason in it,
And not last beyond a minute.
If to further lengths it go,
It does into malice grow.

—Charles Lamb[8]

A man who is never mad or angry can never be passionately in
favor of anything either. A man who never loses his temper might
have nothing worthwhile to lose at all.

—Henri Nouwen[9]

For Your Consideration

- Does your anger ever frighten you? Why might that be?
- Do you judge and criticize yourself for getting angry?
- What do you make of the statement, "Anger comes when there is
  a discrepancy between what we expect and what is real"?
- Do you sometimes cover up your anger? What does that feel
  like? What does it look like in your body?
- What parts of dementia caregiving trigger your anger?
- Describe your anger using a metaphor. Maybe it's a volcano, or a
  tidal wave, or smoldering coals. Use your imagination.
- What good comes from your anger?
- Have you gotten angry at God? What was that like?

Chapter Twelve

• • • • • •

Anxiety

Friends tell me I'm a bit plucky. I have walked into places where wise angels might fear to tread, oblivious to potentially bad outcomes: doing public health nursing in ghettos, leaving a regular job for a new career path with soft money, moving to a community two thousand miles away where I didn't know a soul. I was up for challenges, even thrived on them.

That is how I began dementia caregiving, confident of being able to manage the situation by collecting information, using connections, and securing any needed help. I defied this new challenge to change our life: "Go ahead, dementia, try to knock us down. I dare you!"

Such brashness waned quickly as I encountered the demands of dementia caregiving. I discovered how many things caused me to hesitate, made me less confident and less bold. It wasn't full-blown fear or panic, but rather a sibling—anxiety—that roosted in me. "What if I make bad decisions on Tom's behalf?" "What if I can't continue to earn a paycheck?" "What if my depression comes back?" "What if Tom becomes violent?" "How much is all this stress shortening my life?" "How would I ever again find things to love when I had no one with whom to share the joy?" I worried about every potential problem despite knowing, on some level, that the myriad of scary prospects could not possibly all happen.

There were so many unknowns along this twisted path. I feared what might come roaring around the next turn, clearly doing what my mother had advised against—"borrowing trouble." The psalmist had spoken to me over and over again about walking through the valley of the shadow of death and fearing no evil, but it wasn't evil I feared on this dementia death march. It was the apparent impossibility of caring for Tom while also preserving my own life that frightened me. Every angel in scripture spoke to me the same line—"Be not afraid!"—but clearly there is something in life to be afraid of or we would not be repeatedly admonished to forego fear.

Reflections

Fear and anxiety are related but not exactly the same. Fear is the apprehension we feel when there is realistic, concrete danger in front of us. Fear prepares our bodies to act to protect us and what we love. Anxiety, on the other hand, is the apprehension we feel for things less tangible and more ill-defined, drawn not from the here-and-now but from our memories of the past or our anticipated future. Anxiety lives in our minds, but transfers to our bodies as adrenaline and cortisol swirling in our blood. The intensity of anxiety ranges from slight apprehension all the way to sheer dread.

We dementia caregivers experience a lot of anxiety. One study showed a 44 percent higher prevalence of anxiety in us than in other long-term caregivers.[1] So many things make us fearful and anxious, even though each thing by itself might be of little consequence. But these small things accumulate and become overwhelming. It's hard to name this aggregation, and because it is hard to name, it is also hard to face.

Maybe it does have a name: *fear of the unknown*. Our society disdains the unknown. It wants and expects answers, preferably clear, concise ones. The unknown is seen as an enemy to be conquered, something an intelligent human being should be able to attack and vanquish. Faced with this social norm, it takes uncommon courage to claim that we don't know, can't know, and won't know about something until the future becomes the present. We tend to prefer our known suffering to an uncertain future. Anxiety may be familiar and thus give a false and distorted security. By not naming and addressing our fear of the unknown, we continue to feed it and let it take hold of us, making us more anxious and increasing our suffering.

Naming that we fear the unknown is the first step in releasing its grasp and diminishing its power; it is an act of bravery and daring. Parsing out our accumulated anxiety into its component parts, exploring just what those bits are, and digging around our feelings and memories to find out where they come from—all this gives us what control is possible over an unpredictable future.

The writer of the First Letter of John in the Christian Testament says, "Perfect love casts out fear" (4:18). Loving the unknown is not easy, but the unknown holds the potential for good things as well as hard things. This wisdom calls us to have faith—faith in life, in God, in the Universe. Can we love our fears? Dare we welcome and converse with our anxieties? The unknown won't go away, but the power held by fearing the unknown can start to diminish. We can become more fearless as we engage the elegant beauty and honesty of saying, "I don't know."

Wisdom

Perhaps everything that frightens us is, in its deepest essence, something helpless that wants our love. So you mustn't be frightened, if a sadness rises in front of you, larger than any you have ever seen; if an anxiety, like light and cloud-shadows, moves over your hands and over everything you do. You must realize that something is happening to you, that life has not forgotten you, that it holds you in its hand and will not let you fall.

—Rainer Maria Rilke[2]

Fear of the Lord is the beginning of wisdom, but love from the Lord is its completion.

—William D. Eisenhower[3]

It's often somewhat
Disconcerting when
God takes us at our word.
"Take me and use me,"
We say, meaning it;
But when God does,
There is a moment of surprise,
Perhaps terror, "Me?"

Then, our "Yes" loved from us,
Comes the realization
That the opportunity is gift,
The outcome held in grace.

—Ann Lewin[4]

For Your Consideration

- List the things you fear might happen in your dementia caregiving. Is it probable, even possible, that all these fears will come to pass?
- Which of the things you fear are more likely to actually happen? If they do, where will you turn for help?
- Is acknowledging that we cannot know the future in any way comforting? How so?
- Which would you find preferable: acknowledging that the future is a mystery or rehearsing "what if" scenarios that may or may not occur?
- Is there an alternative to worrying? What is it?
- What are some of the things you can never know for sure?

Chapter Thirteen

• • • • • •

Blame

I can be very good at blaming. Anything. Anyone. When it came to Tom's dementia, I started with blaming his father, whose family history was rampant with Alzheimer's. But it quickly dawned on me that blaming his dad would require I dismiss all the good genes, the ones that made Tom intelligent and handsome. Blaming my father-in-law would discount the rich range of opportunities and experiences he had given Tom, all of which helped make Tom the person I loved.

Then I turned to blaming God for reneging on the pact I thought we had: I'd be good and God would answer my prayers in the affirmative. But I recoiled from blaming God, fearing that I might make God a bit angry, and lose any divine favor I had enjoyed. My perspective of God changed with time, but early in my caregiving I felt that chiding God was not safe, making God a poor target for my criticism.

Then I blamed football. Tom played tackle football in junior high, was a state all-star player in high school, and chose to continue playing throughout college. He loved the game. I wonder if he would have loved it as much if he had known what we know now about traumatic brain injury increasing the risk of dementia and about repeated head injuries probably increasing the risk of cognitive impairment. I'll never know, but I do know that he loved football.

Later I blamed the counselor who didn't recognize Tom's symptoms when early treatment might have kept Tom functioning at a higher level for longer. I blamed the doctor in the first care home that Tom lived in for not taking his painful symptoms seriously when they were actually a rare side effect from a newly prescribed antipsychotic drug.

Once I finished that litany of who to blame, I had a last resort: myself. Where had I missed the hints of dementia? When had I been blind? What could I have done differently—nonaluminum deodorant? More turmeric? A prolonged course of anti-inflammatory medicines? I blamed myself for failing to relieve Tom's suffering and for almost everything else that didn't go well.

What did all of this blaming accomplish? Nothing.

Reflections

Westerners are raised on the scientific method and believe strongly in cause-and-effect, expecting it to suit every situation. It is implicit in our language: *because, since, therefore, hence, as a result, consequently, due to.* Cause-and-effect is in the air we breathe. But life isn't really that simple. It's filled with multiple interrelated causes and risk factors, and with the interplay of numerous phenomena. Cause-and-effect matters in many parts of life, but when it leads dementia caregivers to blaming, it's not helpful.

Blame tries to help us cope by projecting and displacing our feelings onto something or someone else. It fuels a sense of self-righteousness and personal purity. It gives us a false sense of control, and it works until it doesn't. Blame doesn't change the "is-ness" of things, nor does it change the circumstances that created that "is-ness." Whatever the cause, and however hard we try to find something to blame, dementia powerfully moves on, leaving in its wake a ruined brain.

Blame lets us avoid a truth we don't want to face, but sooner or later, we have to face what we have been trying so hard to deny: There is no one to blame for dementia. We cannot point the finger at anyone or anything, and certainly not at ourselves. We find ourselves helpless, and we also see the helplessness of those we have depended on—the doctors and researchers, the spiritual guides we have trusted for answers, even our God. The helplessness we have greatly feared and bitterly fought is at our doorstep

It's both painful and humbling to face our powerlessness. But doing so teaches us the uncomfortable truth that we are human and mortal. We have limited power or control. The best we can do is to manage what we can of our own lives and pay attention to our responses to what life brings us. We may be helpless to stop dementia, but we are not helpless when it comes to caring and loving.

Wisdom

I think this is the hardest lesson about AD [Alzheimer's disease] for the caregiver: you can never do enough to make a difference in the course of the disease. . . . In the end, all those judgments, those self-judgments, are pointless. The disease is inexorable, cruel. It scoffs at everything. . . . It is costly, emotionally, to watch someone move inevitably, step by step, into a dementing illness, and it's hard not to want to blame someone—ourselves most of all. But it is useless.

—Sue Miller[1]

. . . Which is worse, I wonder,
self-blame or innocence?
If I alone caused the accident
despite my zealous swerving
then sheer madness ruled.
But suppose I didn't make it happen?
A more terrifying thought.
Then I can't make it unhappen
and I must accept how brittle,
how utterly helpless we are
despite will, wish, or reason,
always shadowed by danger
in a rampaging world.

—Diane Ackerman[2]

I witnessed a strange trial. Three rabbis, all erudite and pious men, decided one evening to indict God for allowing His children to be massacred. I remember: I was there, and I felt like crying. But there nobody cried. The trial lasted several nights. Witnesses were heard, evidence was gathered, conclusions were drawn, all of which issued finally in a unanimous verdict: The Lord God Almighty, Creator of Heaven and Earth, was found guilty of crimes against creation and humankind. And then, after what seemed like an infinity of silence, the Talmudic scholar looked at the sky and said, "It's time for evening prayers," and the members of the tribunal recited Marriv, the evening service.

—Elie Wiesel[3]

For Your Consideration

- As you witness your loved one's dementia, who or what have you blamed? Who or what do you blame now?
- How does blaming serve you as a dementia caregiver?
- Consider how blaming might be a way to avoid your sadness.
- How have you used blame to compensate for helplessness?
- If there is no one or nothing to blame, where does that leave you? How does that feel?
- Ackerman asks which is worse, self-blame or personal innocence. "Suppose I didn't make it happen" she wonders, realizing "then I can't make it unhappen." For you, is self-blame or personal innocence preferable? Can you say why?

Chapter Fourteen

• • • • • •

Depression

When driving on a highway one day, I briefly considered putting the car into cruise control at seventy miles an hour and taking my hands off the steering wheel, imagining that death was preferable to the life I was living. Before my depression got to that level, there were signs, signs I dismissed as just normal parts of the job of dementia caregiving: fatigue, weight gain, loneliness, forgoing hobbies, withdrawal. The happy face I put on at work didn't always carry over into my other job of caring for Tom.

When the full impact of my depression hit, my bishop agreed that I was in no shape to function as a pastor. She encouraged me to take a medical leave in the form of short-term disability. I was both relieved and embarrassed. My self-image was that I was a very competent person who could weather all storms, not as someone who was disabled. Disabled by a visible physical limitation might have been different, but a mental disability just didn't suit my pride.

Word got around the congregation and the diocese that I was depressed. I imagined that the whole world knew I was unable to function. In truth, I had no idea what others thought of me or my situation. Were they saying, "Jean has cracked up"? Or were they saying, "Good for her. Jean is taking care of herself"? It didn't matter. I was depressed and needed time to heal.

I had to explain my condition to the people who managed the short-term disability plan. Phone in hand, I paced and sobbed as I tried to tell a complete stranger what was happening to me. I was loud and angry, and incredulous that anyone could imagine that in my condition I could care for anyone else. To an onlooker, it would have looked like melodrama, but it was real life, my real life. The man on the other end of the line got the message that I was not capable of working.

A parish nurse friend recommended a psychiatrist for medication and suggested I find respite care for Tom, which I did with her help. Medication was prescribed; it wasn't magic, but it did start to do its job in relatively short order. I found a therapist who also had experience as a spiritual director. I started to relax a bit, knowing that I could sleep without setting the alarm, that I had done something constructive for myself, and that I was hiding nothing. My life was out in the open for people to gossip about if they chose to. It no longer mattered to me.

Reflections

Depression is described by many people using similar words: self-denigrating worthlessness, immobilizing lethargy, uncontrollable crying, an eternal gray fog. It's important to clarify that there's a difference between feeling depressed and having depression. Feeling sadness, loneliness, and grief are part of being human. Most of the time, someone who feels depressed can continue to function and will eventually return to feeling normal. But when a person has clinical depression, the unpleasant feelings linger, are excessive, and interfere with everyday life.

Clinical depression has many of the same characteristics of chronic sorrow. Based on the presenting symptoms, it is difficult to distinguish between them. From the therapist's perspective, making the distinction may be necessary both to appreciate the context of the symptoms and to assure that medical insurance will reimburse for the treatment. From the perspective of the dementia caregiver, the distinction might be significant because of the stigma still attached to mental illness. People might still be more willing to sympathize with someone's sadness than they would be to relate to someone's psychological diagnosis.

Before sharing the dire statistics related to depression in dementia caregivers, I need to humbly say that I question if they are reliable. Why? First, because the distinction between chronic sorrow and depression is difficult to discern. Second, researchers use ambiguous terminology to describe the dementia caregiver's situation, using terms like *caregiver distress, personal role strain, caregiver depression,* and *caregiver burden.* Third, the research that is done lacks a unifying conceptual framework that would assure apples are compared with apples, not oranges. Lastly, data can be distorted due to the understandable inability of the dementia caregivers who are research subjects to clearly distinguish between feeling depressed and experiencing clinical depression. Caregivers report their subjective perceptions and can't be totally objective in their self-reporting. With the above caveat, I share the statistics:

- 30 to 40 percent of family caregivers who care for people with dementia suffer from depression, compared with 5 to 17 percent of noncaregivers of similar ages.[1]
- Female dementia caregivers are disproportionately affected with depression.[2]
- Depression is higher among dementia caregivers than other caregivers, such as those who provide help to individuals with schizophrenia (20 percent) or stroke (19 percent).[3]
- Dementia caregivers of spouses have two and a half times higher odds of having depression than caregivers of people who were not spouses.[4]

In 2003, Kenneth Covinsky *et al.* sought to determine which characteristics of the person with dementia are associated with depression in their caregivers. They identified characteristics of the loved one that are independently associated with a higher risk of caregiver depression:

- Younger age
- White or Hispanic ethnicity compared to African-American ethnicity
- More advanced disease process
- Need for more help with activities of daily living, and
- Behavioral problems, especially anger or aggressiveness.[5]

Covinsky also looked at characteristics of the caregiver as they related to depression. These characteristics included being female, being related to the patient (the highest being a wife), living with the patient, and giving care from 40 to 79 hours a week. (You might wonder if religion can help ward off depression. The jury is still out on that.[6])

Research on the many aspects of caregiver depression is increasing, but for now, all we have are statistical relationships and correlations, with no clear proof of any cause and effect. Caregiver depression can only be understood by a complete understanding of both the person with dementia and the caregiver in their cultural context. Anything less is guesswork.

A friend who has suffered with clinical depression claims, "It's not a breakdown. It's a breakthrough." If having depression causes you to get medication and talk therapy, this can truly be a breakthrough. Medication can help alleviate some of the painful symptoms while you learn new coping strategies and experiment with them. Pills are likely not to be needed once those learnings are established. Talk therapy allows for insight and changing outgrown attitudes learned long ago for other situations. A breakthrough means growth.

Wisdom

What's madness but nobility of soul
At odds with circumstances?

—Theodore Roethke[7]

I know what my heart is like
Since your love died:
It is like a hollow ledge
Holding a little pool
Left there by the tide,
A little tepid pool,
Drying inward from the edge.

—Edna St. Vincent Millay[8]

You have been wounded in many ways. The more you open yourself to being healed, the more you will discover how deep your wounds are. You will be tempted to become discouraged, because under every wound you uncover you will find others. . . . But do not be afraid. The simple fact that you are more aware of your wounds shows that you have sufficient strength to face them.

—Henri Nouwen[9]

But in the darkest, meanest things
There alway, alway something sings.

'Tis not in the high stars alone,
Nor in the cup of budding flowers . . . ,
But in the mud and scum of things
There alway, alway something sings.

—Ralph Waldo Emerson[10]

For Your Consideration

- How does your experience compare with the statistics about caregiver depression?
- If you have felt depressed, use a metaphor to describe it. (Mine was trudging through ankle-deep mud.) Does your metaphor give you any new information?
- If you have been depressed, how have you sought to address your situation? Who and what has helped you?
- If you have experienced depression and not sought help, what is behind that decision?
- Identify one person who could serve as your lifeline if you were to become depressed.
- Do you agree with Emerson that "in the mud and scum" something always sings? If so, name a small, positive outcome that can come from depression.

Chapter Fifteen

• • • • • •

Doubt

Though I have doubted often, I do not sense that doubting is passing judgement on the veracity of a thing. It was more like wondering if a different story or outcome were just as likely, given the information at hand. Doubting is simply allowing for an alternative explanation. It feels normal when the stakes aren't too high, when I can live with whatever outcome presents itself. The only doubting that worried me was doubting my God.

Earlier in my life, my doubt about a God who performed illogical miracles that couldn't be replicated was resolved when I understood that the stories of miracles were told as a means of communicating deep truths, not necessarily facts. But Tom's dementia brought up a bigger doubt about my God.

I doubted that God was all love and only love. Although I had given up the notion that life was fair, I wanted to hold on to the idea that love ultimately ruled the universe and that eventually good would prevail. Good was clearly not prevailing for Tom. Dementia was robbing him of his mobility, his personality, his ability to reflect, and his self-expression. When so much was taken from him, even his smile, I didn't see a God of love ruling the world. I did see the suffering of a humble man who had sought to live his life in love with his God and the beloved Earth.

Even as I questioned a God whose elemental character was only love, I could see God and love in Tom's caregivers. I could see the gift in Tom's dementia as it gave the staff a new perspective; they were unaccustomed to caring for a relatively young, strapping. six-foot-two and otherwise healthy male patient. I could see God expressed in his family and friends. But even as Tom received love, he lived in the inescapable terror of hallucinations. Where was the love in that? Where was God in that?

Reflections

In many religious circles, doubt has a bad reputation. To question God is seen as disloyal, if not downright heretical. In *Doubt in Perspective*, Alister McGrath says, "Admitting to doubt seems to amount to insulting God." As a consequence, doubts get suppressed and become a shield and armor against new information or ideas. McGrath goes on to note that "doubt is not skepticism—the decision to doubt everything deliberately as a matter of principle. . . . Doubt is not unbelief—the decision not to have faith in God. Unbelief is an act of the will rather than a difficulty in understanding."[1] To doubt, however, is to hesitate: to seek understanding before coming to a conclusion.

Faith and doubt are often placed as opposing poles on a continuum and seen as antithetical to each other. But maybe that's not what religion really teaches. Maybe it would be better to create two different continua with different poles.

The first continuum would be *certainty* and *doubt*. Certainty is seen as the measure of orthodoxy and doesn't invite questions. Certainty can cause us to lie to ourselves when there is a collision between a new experience and an old belief. No serious discussion can happen when rigid certainty can't bend. Certainty can shatter when questioned. Doubt, on the other hand, forgoes the security of conviction. It lets us grow and expand. Doubt encourages our curiosity and wonderment. As we walk with our doubts, they offer comfort simply from their honesty and openness.

The other continuum would be *faith* and *creed*. To have a creed is to have an ideology expressed in doctrine and maybe even in dogma. The beliefs are reasoned and formalized. Faith, on the other hand, in the words of the Christian Testament, "is the substance of things hoped for, the evidence of things not seen" (Heb. 11:1, KJV). Faith is not commitment to a belief system but confidence in a reality we cannot see. We are not called to live by certainty but by trust in something bigger than ourselves. Faith is trusting that what can't be proven or predicted just might be possible. We can't live fully by adhering to tenets and intellectual beliefs; rather, we live in a sea of faith, trusting that what doesn't make sense might or might not someday become clear. Faith is walking in the dark. It is moving ahead even when we don't have the whole picture. It can at times be unnerving and at other times immensely consoling.

Beside the doubts that may arise about our understanding of God, dementia caregivers also face the issue of self-doubt. We have been called to take on a very unfamiliar role, and naturally we doubt our abilities. We've had little if any education about how to do it. We were not vetted for our suitability to the tasks and are not given a job description, a timeline, or a mentor. No wonder we doubt that we can handle the job!

For many caregivers, self-doubt is short-lived. It has to be, because there isn't the time or energy to engage in self-doubt. We hit the ground running. We have to make decision after decision and perform task after task, doing our level best to just put one foot ahead of the other. We make choices based on the best information we have at the time and use our best judgment. Though we make mistakes, they aren't fatal and we soon learn that the sun always rises the next day. Grounded in our daily experience we develop backbone and grow in courage. We come to learn that our mistakes are somehow balanced by our successes. Our caregiving, we find, may not be perfect, but it is good enough. Tenacity, perseverance, and grit give us confidence in our caring. We learn to rely on our compassion for ourselves and for those we love in order to get us through.

Wisdom

From the place where we are right
flowers will never grow
in the Spring.

The place where we are right
is hard and trampled
like a yard.

But doubts and loves
dig up the world
like a mole, a plough.
And a whisper will be heard in the place
where the ruined
house once stood.

—Yehuda Amichai[2]

For nothing worth proving can be proven,
Nor yet disproven: wherefore thou be wise,
Cleave ever to the sunnier side of doubt,
And cling to Faith beyond the forms of Faith!
She reels not in the storm of warring words,
She brightens at the clash of "Yes" and "No,"
She sees the Best that glimmers thro' the Worst,
She feels the Sun is hid but for a night.

—Alfred Lord Tennyson[3]

For Your Consideration

- Has dementia caregiving caused you to question your faith or your lack of faith? Have you had any misgivings one way or the other?
- If doubting is difficult for you, can you identify why that is?
- How has doubt been helpful in your life?
- Do you doubt your abilities as a dementia caregiver? Why is that? How realistic is that?
- How does your faith relate to your self-doubt?
- Do you believe that God can move through your questions and qualms? What life experiences have brought you to this belief?
- Are there some things in life of which you are absolutely certain? What are they?

Chapter Sixteen

• • • • • •

Emptiness

In early evening on a New Year's Day, I was prostrate on the floor in our bedroom, crying uncontrollably and letting my tears soak into the royal blue carpet. Exhaustion had caught up with me, and I let myself collapse. The Christmas season, with its demands for goodwill, cheer, shopping, baking, and church services, had been added to winter's demands for shoveling snow-covered sidewalks and driving on icy roads, and these had topped off the ever-present demands of caring for Tom. They were taking a hefty toll. My energy was gone. I was running on fumes. It was our wedding anniversary: fourteen years married to the man of my dreams, and there I was on the floor, sobbing. I tried to stifle the sound in an effort to not attract Tom's attention from the next room. He didn't need to know that I was "losing it," that I was desolate.

Tom came into the bedroom. His cognitive intelligence was much diminished, but his emotional intelligence remained. He sat quietly on the edge of our bed and eventually found two words to speak, "Nursing home." I wailed. I pulled myself off the floor, sat down next to him, and we held each other as the tears continued to flow.

That moment was proof of my emptiness, something I was hide-bound to deny. Tom was not fooled; only I was. I thought I could go on giving forever—always outpouring good deeds, comforting words, lively energy. (That's what loving partners do, isn't it?) I thought I was taking care of myself by finding snippets of "me time"—taking short walks in the neighborhood, meeting a friend for a cup of coffee now and then, reading some poetry. But these were like a drizzle of rain teasing a drought-stricken land.

I seemed to have two speeds: on and off. When I was on, I gave my all. I was like a fast-moving locomotive, fueled by a fear of stopping. That fear of stopping to take care of myself was born of my mistake in conflating selfishness and self-love. But I could go on no longer. I had to stop.

Reflections

Exhaustion doesn't come to dementia caregivers in one fell swoop. It comes incrementally, like the frog and the hot water: put the frog into boiling water, and it will jump out and save itself, but put it into tepid water and increase the heat slowly and it will die, unaware of the gradual change in temperature.

In dementia caregiving, exhaustion is cumulative. Our energies are expended at constantly increasing rates, at first almost imperceptibly but then faster and faster, until exhaustion becomes the new norm. We become suspended in an eternal now, one day like every other, meeting the daily round and wondering if it will ever end. A numbness sets in as the only way to cope.

In the wisdom of Twelve-Step programs, we need to hit bottom before we can make different choices and move toward health. We need to come to a place where we are incapable of continuing as we have been, being thoroughly bankrupt. It's not a pretty picture, but it's critical. Once at the bottom, we need to sit with our emptiness for a while, repellent and painful as that is. We need to make friends with the emptiness because it is a place full of potential for changing our ways, for coming to grips with our inability to go it alone and for accepting that we are needy human beings made for community. Hitting bottom makes us realize that we are not messiahs. Being selfless and self-denying might sound like attractive character traits, but are they really? If we deny our own selves, how can we give anything really worthwhile to another?

A Twelve-Step aphorism is valuable: "Nothing changes if nothing changes." Changing, though difficult, is holy work. It starts when we ask ourselves hard questions: What is driving the relentless giving? Is it to make us look good, to present ourselves as self-sufficient? Is it to meet some external, unwritten standard? Is it an attempt to garner approval, to shore up our self-image by courting praise? Is it the pride of thinking we are the only ones who can give adequate care to the one we love? Is it a belief that the one being cared for is more important than the one doing the caring?

We all have unexamined beliefs about selfishness and self-love. Selfishness is lacking consideration for other people and being concerned excessively with one's own personal profit or pleasure. That hardly describes a person who is a caregiver. Self-love, on the other hand, is not selfishness. Spiritual wisdom tells us to love others *as* we love ourselves, not *instead* of ourselves. We need to love ourselves and to act on that healthy self-love with self-respect. We need to be compassionate with ourselves, creating healthy boundaries, making wide-enough margins next to the text of our lives to offer ourselves breathing space, making a priority of having our needs (though not all our wants) met.

Can you picture yourself quietly listening to your heart with gentle compassion, staying with pain, withholding all judgement, and taking a tissue when needed? Oh, that we could be such a loving presence to ourselves.

Wisdom

If you want to live an authentic, meaningful life, you need to master the art of disappointing and upsetting others, hurting feelings, and living with the reality that some people just won't like you. It may not be easy, but it's essential.

—Cheryl Richardson[1]

Yesterday I was clever, so I wanted to change the world.
Now I am wise, so I am changing myself.

—Rumi[2]

Self-care is never a selfish act—it is simply good stewardship of the only gift I have, the gift I was put on Earth to offer others. Anytime we can listen to true self and give the care it requires, we do it not only for ourselves, but for the many others whose lives we touch.

—Parker Palmer[3]

The man who is wise . . . will see his life more as a reservoir than a canal. The canal simultaneously pours out what it receives; the reservoir retains the water till it is filled, then discharges the overflow without loss to itself. . . . Today there are many . . . who act as canals; the reservoirs are far too rare. . . . You must learn to await this fullness before pouring out your gifts. Do not try to be more generous than God.

—Bernard of Clairvaux[4]

For Your Consideration

- Recall a time when you felt selfish for putting yourself first. Describe the situation. Describe how you felt inside.
- Do you feel selfish when you seek to meet your own needs?
- Does feeling guilty diminish the benefit of the time spent focusing on your own self-care? How would it have felt to be "guilt-free"?
- How does your body feel when you are exhausted? What hurts? Metaphorically, what is your body telling you when it's feeling this way?
- What does "enough" mean when it comes to dementia caregiving?
- We often imagine there is a right way to care, a standard we must meet. Who defines "good enough" caregiving for you?
- Consider the quote from Bernard of Clairvaux and ponder how your reservoir can be filled. Identify small things that fill you up and bring you a moment of pleasure or relaxation. Can these help you to be a reservoir, discharging the overflow without loss to yourself?

Chapter Seventeen

• • • • • •

Forgiveness

Before his disease fully took over his brain, Tom and I would talk about how dementia was reconstructing our lives, taking us from the path we intended and leading us to places we didn't want to go. Tom spoke of how he wanted to live out his days in the familiarity of the home we had made together. But we acknowledged that his wishes might not be possible to carry out, and we dared to talk about what it would mean if we had to live apart.

Tom said words I haven't forgotten: "Alzheimer's will kill me, but I don't want it to kill you too." The words hung in the air till we wept at the poignant beauty and lavish gift that those words were. He went on to say he didn't want us separated and certainly dreaded a nursing home, clearly realizing that living apart would add to his suffering. But he recognized the reality that late-stage dementia would be too much for any one person to manage. He knew our finances couldn't support around-the-clock care at home. Separation wouldn't be a measure of our love. It would simply be a practicality. Tom knew the severe demands of dementia caregiving from his father's dementia, and he knew he wouldn't be leaving our home unless my caring for him was killing me. His leaving home would likely be at a time when he no longer had words or logic. At that future time, he wouldn't be able to offer me forgiveness for separating us, for my acting to protect my life rather than meeting his need for security and comfort. He forgave me in advance.

Those words, "I don't want Alzheimer's to kill you too," became a mantra to me when Tom moved into full-time dementia care years later. I remembered the earlier Tom and silently repeated his words of pardon each time I left him at the care home, knowing that every leaving meant fresh abandonment to him and that loneliness and fear were his ever-present and malicious companions. I repeated his forgiveness, over and over again. Tom had taught me much about the unself-interested, unquestioning love that makes forgiveness possible.

Reflections

We dementia caregivers need to forgive ourselves for the mistakes we inevitably make. Bad decisions and hurtful actions are a painful part of life, and they don't stop just because we become dementia caregivers. The distress we cause is not intentional, but nonetheless can result in suffering. It can be a challenge to forgive ourselves.

Religions teach that we can be absolved of our mistakes. Charles Wesley's hymn tells that God "breaks the power of cancelled sin." We are forgiven. Yet many religious people seem to give only lip service to being forgiven and don't live their lives as thankful, forgiven people. Some wallow in their transgressions, real or imagined, and fail to accept absolution. Many apparently believe a person must be worthy of forgiveness, and that forgiveness is not really a free gift. We live in a society that has trouble believing that we can be unworthy and forgiven at the same time. But such a belief betrays hubris, an underlying attitude that we are more clever than a God who forgives with no strings attached.

In the Gospels, forgiveness precedes confession and repentance. God chooses to forgive us. It is in light of that grace that we dare to confess. "Confession is good for the soul," of course, but confession is not just *mea culpa*, nor is it a way to punish ourselves. Much more importantly, it is truth-telling. And we know that truth can set us free. Confessing can help heal our souls.

Confessing can be done to the one we have offended, whether or not that person fully comprehends what we are saying. It can be done with a confessor or a good friend who listens well and loves us through the ordeal of speaking the truth that we'd prefer not to acknowledge. Maybe confession could even be done to a blank wall. Confession is simply telling the truth, and that is a big part of learning to forgive ourselves.

As well as forgiving ourselves, we need to forgive the one we care for, forgiving the wrongs done to us intentionally or unintentionally. Every long-term relationship has its list of wrongs, large and small. Some offenses may be egregious and make forgiveness exceptionally hard. If abuse or violence has been part of the way we have been wronged, there are multiple layers that need to be considered. Developing dementia does not make a person into a saint.

If the one we care for had a healthy brain, there might be time to rebuild trust and create a stronger and mutually loving relationship. But a person with advancing dementia is not capable of processing the past or grasping how prior deeds have hurt us. Even less can they express remorse or volitionally change. That, however, ought not keep us holding on to old grudges. Withholding forgiveness holds us in a useless cycle.

A wise nun once told me that I needed to forgive by acting in ways that demonstrate that I had already forgiven. In other words, by practicing and acting out forgiveness, I would one day find that I had actually forgiven. Much happens when the internal, resentful posture changes, and I found she was right.

Forgiving is not being naïve. It does not undo the offensive deed. It does not do away with the hope for justice. It is not forgetting. Forgiveness does, however slowly, loosen the hold that the past has on the present.

Wisdom

To forgive is to set a prisoner free and discover that the prisoner was you.

—Lewis B. Smedes[1]

Forgiveness means we are not destined endlessly to play the grievances of yesterday. It is the ability to live with the past without being held captive to the past. It would not be an exaggeration to say that forgiveness is the most compelling testimony to human freedom. It is about the action that is not reaction. It is the refusal to be defined by circumstance. It represents our ability to change course, reframe the narrative of the past, and create an unexpected set of possibilities for the future.

—Rabbi Jonathan Sacks[2]

My dear children, let's not just talk about love; let's practice real love. This is the only way we'll know we're living truly, living in God's reality. It's also the way to shut down debilitating self-criticism, even when there is something to it. For God is greater than our worried hearts and knows more about us than we do ourselves.

—1 John 3:20, *The Message*

He who is devoid of the power to forgive is devoid of the power to love. There is some good in the worst of us and some evil in the best of us.

—Martin Luther King Jr.[3]

For Your Consideration

- Do you find it difficult to forgive yourself? Why do you suppose that is?
- Identify a situation where you find it hard to forgive yourself. Imagine asking yourself for forgiveness and receiving it. How does that feel?
- Is it harder to forgive your loved one than it is to forgive yourself, or *vice versa*? Explore that.
- Is there an old offense that you hold on to? How do you feel as you recall it? If those feelings provide some benefit for you, describe that. What might it feel like to release it?

- What would conditional forgiving look like? Can true forgiveness be conditional?
- How do you feel when someone forgives you?
- What is your experience of confession? If confession is simply truth-telling, what truth could you tell that would help you feel free inside? Can you speak it out loud in privacy, or write it down?

Chapter Eighteen

• • • • • •

Grief

The heartache I experienced in caring for Tom was a low ostinato, a persistent background sound underlying so much of what occupied my days. Sadness was just that pervasive. There was nothing piercing or shocking about the grief; it was just insidious and constant. I wondered if this bleakness was what I had heard about in nursing school, something called *anticipatory grief*—the sadness a person experiences before the actual death of a loved one. Unconsciously, I hoped it was, and that all this grief before Tom's death would somehow amount to "paying forward" so that there would be less grief when he did die.

That didn't happen. My grief wasn't anticipating Tom's inevitable death; it was about things that were happening in the present. I lamented so many seemingly small diminishments: Tom's inability to manage the score in a Scrabble game, his inability to read a map and guide me while I drove, his inability to figure out how to walk up the stairs. Most stunning to the gardener in me was his inability to dig a hole in the ground so I could plant a tree. He didn't recognize what the shovel was to be used for, what a "hole" meant, or what the relationship was between the bare root tree and the words I was saying.

I was living with Tom's regularly occurring, ever new losses. His losses were mine too. Most of these were invisible to others who couldn't see how these losses changed our daily lives, nor did they have to adapt to them and accept them. But we did.

The sadness that had been building inside me would burst its gates in my counselor's office. It was as though I collected the sorrow in a huge cistern and could safely empty it in a great flood when I was with her. It was in this wailing that I experienced something resembling a ritual of mourning.

Reflections

Grief is a very natural and uncontrollable response to loss. It's the emotional suffering you endure when something or someone you love is taken away. The more significant the loss, the more intense the grief will be. New losses recall old losses, so there's a cumulative effect as well.

Grief seldom comes alone. It is multifaceted, one of those "cluster" emotions that is a conglomerate of other feelings. It can come with anger, guilt, or fear. One feeling that may unexpectedly appear in the mix with grief is relief, such as when the person you care for stops driving a car, or when the dementia is so advanced that they are no longer aware of forgetting. These are losses, but with a welcomed aspect.

We know grief when we see it and feel it—tears, disturbed sleep, lack of energy, changes in appetite, lethargy, withdrawal. Many people are familiar with Elisabeth Kubler-Ross's five stages of grief—denial, anger, bargaining, depression, and acceptance—and believe them to be sequential, but they are more cyclical than linear. Stages recur. They can come out of sequence. Early in her last book, she said the five stages of grief "were never meant to help tuck messy emotions into neat packages. They are responses to loss that many people have, but there is not a typical response to loss, as there is no typical loss. Our grieving is as individual as our lives."[1] "Correct grieving" can't be planned or prescribed because there is no correct way to grieve. There's only your way. And mine.

Research has recently emerged about the grief experience of dementia caregivers. To the already substantial compendium of types of grief (such as anticipatory grief, ambiguous loss, and prolonged grief disorder), some newer terms have begun to appear. I share them here, not because intellectualizing grief is a good way to handle it (it isn't), but because these descriptions might affirm your experience and give context to your feelings.

One newer phrase is *disenfranchised grief*, grief that is inhibited and not expressed freely. Disenfranchised grief is influenced, according to the research by Jude Weir, by three factors:

- Social norms that dictate what's acceptable grief, how long mourning can take, and who can mourn. (Psychological losses associated with dementia caregiving are not commonly recognized as losses worthy of grief.)
- Erosion of the relationship between caregiver and the loved one with dementia, making it impossible to grieve together or resolve issues, past or current.
- Stigma, shame, and secrecy still associated with dementia.[2]

Many of our losses are invisible to the world we live in. They become ghostlike yet certainly real to us.

Another newer phrase is *dementia grief*, or *predeath grief*. Allison Lindauer and Teresa Harvath combed forty-nine peer-reviewed papers and two from popular media. They found that "pre-death grief in the context of dementia caregiving is a meaningful concept found in the popular media [but] from a scholarly point of view, it is an emerging concept."[3] Why is dementia grief distinct? Because:

- The loved one with dementia suffers a psychological death prior to a physical death.
- There is a long and uncertain trajectory of the disease process.
- Communication between the dementia caregiver and the person with dementia is sorely compromised.
- The quality of the relationship, family roles, and caregiver freedom are significantly changed.[4]

A third term I found useful is *chronic sorrow*. It is used to describe the experience of parents of children with congenitally debilitating conditions. It also has application to the dementia caregiver experience.

Susan Roos has written extensively on chronic sorrow, and proposes this definition:

> A set of pervasive, profound, continuing, and recurring grief responses resulting from a significant loss or absence of crucial aspects of . . . another living person to whom there is deep attachment. The essence of chronic sorrow is a painful discrepancy between what is perceived as reality and what continues to be dreamed of. The loss is ongoing since the source of the loss continues to be present. The loss is a living loss.[5]

For dementia caregivers, this is the loss of the life we expected and the relationship we hoped to continue. Our dreams are dashed as we live loss. Chronic sorrow, say the experts, cannot be resolved. It is to be endured, yet in naming it, we begin to live more peaceably with it.

Ignoring grief does not make it go away, no matter how hard we try to distract or busy ourselves. Denying it only gives it strength. So what are we to do? We might start by giving up the idea of "normal" grieving. It doesn't exist. Then we might explore ways of sharing our story. Face-to-face support is important, like meeting with a support group or a counselor. We need to have a witness to our loss and tell others what we feel, want, and need. Simply verbalizing our experience gives a modicum of control over it. We might even try talking directly to our loved one whether or not they can comprehend what we are saying. Maybe we could write a letter to them, even though it will never be read.

Doing what we can to take care of ourselves physically also helps equip us to handle the sadness that comes. A counselor suggested I set aside regular time to weep. Making space and time for crying gave me a message about the legitimacy of the feeling. It gave me a way to honor the grief. Sometimes I used the time for journaling, other times for ranting and raving, and other times for simply weeping. Giving attention to grief helps it become more like waves lapping at the shore and less like a tsunami.

There's an ancient Chinese proverb that shares this wisdom: When you are grieving, you are meeting a dragon. If you ignore the dragon, it will eat you. If you try to confront the dragon, it will overpower you. But if you ride the dragon, you will take advantage of its might and power. Do whatever you can do to get the grief out of your head and into your heart. Mourn. Tears come from the heart, not the brain. They cleanse from the inside.

Wisdom

Ah, Grief, I should not treat you
like a homeless dog
who comes to the back door
for a crust, for a
meatless bone.
I should trust you.
I should coax you
into the house and give you
your own corner,
a worn mat to lie on,
your own water dish.
You think I don't know you've been living
under my porch.
You long for your real place to be readied
before winter comes. You need
your name,
your collar and tag. You need
the right to warn off intruders,
to consider
my house your own
and me your person
and yourself
my own dog.

—Denise Levertov[6]

Whenever the clouds cry, green emerges. How can the grass be pleased unless clouds cry? Wherever tears fall, there descends the blessing of God. Shed tears like a moaning waterwheel so that growth will thrive.

—Rumi[7]

Take my mind off these matters,
> But let my heart continue to beat,
Let my soul wherever it resides
> Continue to sing in the rain of falling petals.

—Mark Johnson[8]

No final healing is likely to come from [analyzing your wounds]. You need to let your wounds go down into your heart. Then you live them through and discover that they will not destroy you. Your heart is greater than your wounds.

—Henri Nouwen[9]

For Your Consideration

- Several types of grief have been identified—chronic sorrow, disenfranchised grief, and predeath dementia grief. Do you resonate with any particular one? In what way has that been part of your experience?
- What losses have you experienced as a result of taking on your caregiving role? What dreams have you lost?
- What is your relationship with tears?
- How has your sadness affected other relationships in your life?
- What would you like others to know about how to support you in your grief? Could you tell them what you need or want?
- Are there things you have learned from your losses that you probably wouldn't have learned another way? Have your losses caused you to grow?

Chapter Nineteen

•　•　•　•　•　•

Guilt

Colossal guilt enveloped me when I moved Tom from our familiar home to live in a care facility. I did it for my own sanity and health. The enormous shame of "putting away" a defenseless person flooded me.

The care facility to which Tom moved first was in our neighborhood, but it was light-years away from what he knew. In an effort to make it feel familiar, I furnished it with art from the house, coordinated bed quilt and pillows, and photos of family and friends. But there was so much I couldn't bring: the cardinals and juncos he had fed, the squirrels that had entertained him from the walnut trees, and the wren that sang each morning. I couldn't import the smell of me on the bedsheets, the sight of the sleeping cat curled on the sofa, or the warmth of the wood floor underfoot in the kitchen. These had to stay behind.

I took our marriage vows seriously. "Will you love him, comfort him, honor and keep him, in sickness and in health?" I had responded with a hearty "I will!" I felt I was breaking those promises by living apart and leaving him to his illness. Little did I know then that I could never stop loving him, that comforting him could mean singing him to sleep or sitting with him in silence, that honoring his body would include brushing his teeth and clipping his toenails, or that keeping him would mean advocating for him in a complex health care system and finding creative ways to pay the bills that came from the care home.

But I didn't know that when Tom moved. All I knew was that this separation was horrific for both of us, and I felt guilty. Guilty of betraying him? Guilty of forswearing that big star in my heavenly crown, awarded for sacrificing my life for his? Two years after living apart, when Tom was hospitalized in a geriatric psychiatric unit because his behaviors were too much for the staff at the care home, I again felt guilty. The hospital doctor wrote in Tom's medical record, "His wife is his Valium." That was flattering, but I was well aware I was withholding his much craved "Valium" by not caring for him at home.

My wise daughter-in-law asked if I thought that keeping Tom at home would have caused his illness to stop progressing. I wanted that to be true, but knew it wasn't. The disease would march on no matter where Tom lived. That realization was humbling, as I saw that pride was at the root of my guilt: I fancied that Tom would be happy and stable at home with me. He wouldn't be. He couldn't be. Neither my hubris nor my guilt could save Tom from his fate.

Reflections

How ironic that we dementia caregivers, we who give our very selves in doing the best we can for our loved ones, should feel guilty. Feeling guilt is common in dementia caregivers, as common as feeling grief and anger. It makes no rational sense, but that doesn't stop us. We try, and try harder, to do the right thing, yet we feel ashamed that we haven't done enough. What's that about?

In a sermon, I once heard a preacher say that guilt is like the little red light on the dashboard of a car. It lights up to say, "Something's wrong." It asks for attention. There's nothing wrong with the little red light. It's doing its job. It is not the cause of the problem; it is simply the messenger. It points to the need to look further, to find the cause that might otherwise be hidden from view till it would be too late. It clearly behooves us to look deeper when we find the guilt light blinking.

Bruce Narramore, in his article "Guilt: Where Theology and Psychology Meet," speaks of the psychodynamic origin of guilt. He says the superego is the driver of three selves. The first is the *ideal self*, the center of conscience that contains our values. It is the self we would like to be, and becomes a yardstick by which we measure our behavior. The second is the *corrective self*, the source of healthy guilt. It holds the internalized lessons and admonitions that show us when we have indeed done something wrong. The *punitive self* is the source of unhealthy guilt. Its origin is in perceived threats of punishment and rejection, and this unhealthy guilt can too often drive our behaviors.[1]

Generally, society uses the word *guilt* to mean corrective guilt, the feeling we have when we have crossed a social norm or have misbehaved. It's sometimes called *transgression guilt*. Such guilt is a good thing; it causes us to behave better.

Unhealthy guilt from the ideal self, however, is capable at times of running rampant. It might be called *perfection guilt*, occurring when we don't meet our own high standards, when we do our best but don't get it absolutely, thoroughly, irrefutably right. Perfection is unattainable in dementia caregiving, despite our hypervigilance and hyperresponsibility. Perfection does not exist. Following all the experts' excellent advice will not create a pure and ideal situation for our particular loved ones, in our particular circumstances, every single time. We become our own worst enemy when we try to be perfect, when we seek to be above our own reproach. Being a perfectionist is another form of hubris, or pride. We've often been warned against the deadly sin of pride, but we fail to see how perfectionism is a form of pride. And perfectionism can be deadly.

The punitive self is the source of *inappropriate guilt*, a term used when a person feels responsible for causing negative outcomes when it was actually not their fault. A larger version would be *survivor's guilt*. Inappropriate guilt occurs when we do something that's right and we somehow feel it is wrong.

Just being female brings with it a propensity for feeling inappropriate guilt. Anne Schaef says in *Women's Reality* that women suffer from "the original sin of being born female."[2] There are unwritten social rules for women, and if we don't mind them, we feel that we've done something wrong. Laying down our personal hopes for the benefit of the family is one such unwritten rule. Schaef says that all our good deeds and right actions are not enough to make us fit into a white male society or absolve us of this particular original sin. Society is changing, of course, and women today are likely to have fewer hang-ups about others' expectations of their roles and duties. Many of us, however, were brought up to believe some lies. Courage is needed to rethink what we've been taught and to see these guilt feelings for what they are—inappropriate.

A peculiar kind of inappropriate guilt can come to those of us with religious tendencies. Maybe it could be called *old religion guilt.* It works this way: We pray, but God does not meet our request, so we reason, "It must be me." We wonder if we are not praying hard enough, or long enough. We wonder if we have some secret sin and that's the reason God isn't answering our prayers. R. S. Thomas reflects this old religion guilt in his poem "Emerging,"[3] where the speaker explains God's silence to his prayer by deeming himself unfit. We are not unfit. We are just overreaching, thinking we can change nature, or that we can control the uncontrollable.

What's to be done? We cannot change yesterday, but we might be able to reframe our experience of it. We might come to the realization that we did the best we could, at the time, with the information and feelings we had, and then let guilt go. We might see ourselves not as disloyal but living into a newer loyalty. We might see ourselves not as betraying, but as expressing a new faithfulness based on new circumstances. We might be able to stare down inappropriate guilt, knowing that it no longer serves us or our loved one.

Wisdom

Our feelings of guilt . . . spur us on to bear the pain and do penance. And we do that by means of self-accusation—the magical instrument we use to "settle the accounts" of the past. . . . [They] take no account of what is reasonable. They whisper to us that we could always have done more.

—Huub Buijssen[4]

I need to know I am yours, Beloved,
To untangle my every alliance with guilt.
When that cruel net casts itself,
It can cause even a great one
To live in sorrow and sadness.

—Hafiz[5]

For Your Consideration

- Why do you think guilt is such a universal feeling in caregivers?
- When you feel guilty, how does your body experience it?
- What kind of guilt is most prevalent in your life now?
- If guilt is part of your motivation for caregiving, does it impact the care you give?
- Can you relate to being a perfectionist? To being hypervigilant or hyperresponsible? What positives do you find in perfectionism? What are the pitfalls?
- What's your history with inappropriate guilt? Where did it come from? What would you say to inappropriate guilt now?
- Can you imagine seeing mistakes as opportunities to learn and grow?

Chapter Twenty

• • • • • •

Helplessness

Tom was marginally conscious when I arrived at the care home after work. He had had an excruciating day of vomiting and diarrhea. All that evening and all night, I kept vigil from the chair next to his bed, reading to him, or singing softly, or just being present to him. He slipped deeper into senselessness as the hours wore on. I tried to elicit a response from him, first stroking his face and arms, then using my voice ever more loudly, eventually resorting to rubbing his sternum, a sure way to rouse near comatose patients. But Tom responded to none of it. I dozed on and off and wondered if Tom was leaving this world. He had certainly ventured further than he ever had before.

An aide came into the room at 5:30 a.m. to get him ready for breakfast. I asked if we couldn't just let him rest awhile longer. She agreed, saying, "He looks so peaceful." At 7 a.m. our doctor came in. I was exhausted and fearful of what his answer might be, but I asked the question anyway: "Could we stop feeding Tom and allow him to die with the scant dignity he has left?"

He let my request sink in, and then said, "I'm so sorry, Jean. I can't write that order. I would need the support of the Ethics Committee." Was I hearing resignation in his voice? Or worse, had we just lost our ally?

At 9 a.m. I left Tom, still asleep, and joined the well-groomed professionals assembled around the large board room table. They quickly refrained from the usual coworker banter, silenced by my presence. Our doctor presented the situation succinctly: Tom's lapse into unconsciousness following a day of vomiting and diarrhea, Tom's overall physical condition, and my request that we abstain from rousing or feeding him, knowing this would let him die.

One by one, these people, who had neither touched Tom nor known him before the onset of tangles in his brain, spoke. First was the director of nursing, who knew Tom through reports from the aides; then the CEO whom I had not seen before; then the social worker who came to Tom's unit weekly, but with whom I was yet to have a conversation. These were followed by the chaplain who came on Sundays, the occupational therapist and the speech therapist, who hadn't worked with Tom for over a year.

They said, each in his or her own way, "He is in our care. You have entrusted him to us. There are regulations and protocols we must follow. This would be tantamount to assisted suicide, clearly illegal. We've been through this with other patients. Rest assured that we are doing our best for your loved one. We will not neglect him."

Through my fatigue and unchecked tears, I, as Tom's legal health care representative, presented my case. I reminded them that I had not given Tom to them, but was simply paying them to do what I could no longer do alone at home. I spoke of Tom's sadness at his father's failed suicide attempt, when dementia had prevented his dad from the drowning he had intended by walking into the Charles River with a heavy stone lashed to his body. I told of Tom's support for his mother, who made a clear decision at age ninety-three that her life was complete and she wanted to withdraw hyperalimentation and intravenous hydration. The most convincing evidence I held for last—Tom's request years ago that should he ever develop dementia as his father and aunt and uncle had before him, would I please take him into the Red Desert of Wyoming near his retreat center, walk away, and not come looking for him.

My pleading did nothing more than to prompt them to pass me some Kleenex. Their decision was unanimous. Tom would be fed. These people were not cold-hearted. Nor were they brave.

While the Ethics Committee meeting was taking place, an aide had given Tom a bed bath, dressed him in an oversize T-shirt and stretchy black pants, hoisted him into the air using a hydraulic lift, deposited him in a wheelchair, wheeled him to the dining area, and attempted to feed him pureed pancakes.

Reflections

Encountering helplessness can be demoralizing. It makes us question ourselves, causing us to wonder if we are frauds, people only masquerading as caregivers. We don't know exactly what we are doing, but we do our best in spite of being impotent to stop the disease from progressing. We find that our ineffectual attempts to influence situations leave us exposed and feeble.

Ours is not the "learned helplessness" that counselors treat with empowerment tools. We are very competent and effective in other parts of our lives. This helplessness is different. It is helplessness against a disease, policies, practices, and people more powerful than ourselves. We live within boundaries they have defined and that constrict us. These are not limits of our making or choosing. I suppose if there is a gift in feeling helpless, it is in giving us more sympathy for the weakness and defenselessness experienced by our loved ones with dementia.

Another gift—probably less desired—is that helplessness makes us humble. We are, as a friend quipped, "saved from the hubris and self-deception that we are capable." Society wants us to be capable; we want to be capable. But there are times we are on the wrong side of the tension between having all the resources and having all the need.

We always have some power, even when it is not the kind of power we wanted or expected to wield. At least one holy man, Jesus of Nazareth, lived with what the world sees as powerlessness and he bore it without shame. In an occupied country, with no money or status, without "a place to lay his head," he used the power he did have: his integrity and his willingness to embody faith, honesty, hope, and compassion. When we are emptied of our personal power, we can more easily be filled with grace and power beyond our own making.

Maybe another gift of helplessness is that it gives us an opportune way to revisit our self-identity. We start to acknowledge that though our worldly power may be weak, our inner power can be strong. We see that we are surprisingly capable of living vigorously despite loathsome boundaries others have placed on us. We can actually survive after having to capitulate to forces beyond our control. We learn to say *yes* to what comes, invited or uninvited. We experience compassion and respect for ourselves as we claim our integrity. We see the beauty and strength of our love, fortitude, and persistence—the things that matter most.

We are not responsible for the outcome, but we are responsible for our effort. We are not responsible for success, but we are responsible for our faithfulness.

Wisdom

Full moon is falling through the sky.
Cranes fly through the clouds.
Wolves howl. I cannot find rest
Because I am powerless
To amend a broken world.

—Tu Fu (712–770 CE)[1]

You're blessed when you're at the end of your rope. With less of you there is more of God. . . . You're blessed when you feel you've lost what is most dear to you. Only then can you be embraced by the One most dear to you. You're blessed when you're content with just who you are—no more, no less. That's the moment you find yourselves proud owners of everything that can't be bought.

—Matthew 5:3–5, *The Message*

One man meets with nothing but crosses and disappointments, and thereby gains more than all the world is worth.

—William Law[2]

For Your Consideration

- What thoughts go through your mind when you are faced with helplessness? Choose one and ask yourself if that thought is actually true.
- Do you find that you are more concerned with the result of your caregiving than with the process of your caregiving? What would it be like for you to have your faithfulness in caregiving be more important than the outcome of your caregiving?
- Do you have a habitual way of responding to helplessness? Can you describe it? Can you imagine a different kind of response?
- What does it mean to you to be humble? Can you conceive of moving from being humiliated to being humble when faced with ineffectual advocacy for your loved one?
- What kind of power do you wield as a dementia caregiver? Identify it. Then claim it.
- How does the strength of love show itself in your caregiving?
- Recall a time when someone showed you a small kindness, yet you remember it to this day. How does this inform you about how inconsequential, mundane gestures of kindness matter in life?

Chapter Twenty-One

· · · · · ·

Hope

During Tom's drawn-out illness, I hoped a lot. My hope changed with time and experience. The first real hope I dared to have was in a clinical trial in which Tom participated. I hoped he was not taking the placebo and that there would be a difference in his disease process, that the medicine would slow it, if not cure it. But that trial had to be halted midway through. Too many deaths.

The next big hope came after Tom's move from our home to the memory care facility. There he engaged with some staff and told them about the huge dream catcher made by his Dakota friends hanging on his wall. He invited other residents to see the picture book of his Wyoming retreat center. I hoped this behavior would be a harbinger of the days and months to come—a contented, dignified Tom, living apart from me. But it didn't last, to no one's surprise but mine. Soon Tom realized that this was the place he was to live and not just visit, and it was very foreign. Frustration set in. His anger flared. That hope was short-lived.

Other hopes replaced it. I hoped he would get along with all the staff, and they with him, creating a safe and livable home, if not a joyful one. But no. His size, strength, and anger threatened some staff members; I had to find a different care home.

Dashed as those hopes were, I continued to hope. I hoped his hallucinations would subside with medication. They did not. I hoped that an infection would set in to quicken his death. It did not. Finally, I hoped he would have a peaceful death. That hope was realized.

Reflections

Why, in the face of so many unrealized wishes, do we continue to hope? Maybe hope just happens. It's an energy we do not and cannot conjure that simply drives us forward.

Hope is different from expecting, which is very concrete and has echoes of "should." Hope is lighter, less predictable. Hope is also different from wishing in the same way deep joy is different from happiness. Wishing is more fanciful, ephemeral. We wish upon a star knowing that it's whimsy. Hope is quieter, more akin to yearning and desiring, deeper in the soul, less self-conscious. It has more *maybe* in it.

Leland Beaumont in an online article explores different kinds of hope. His schematic describes the relationship between two forces, or two axes. The first axis, which is vertical, he calls "Outlook," and it is a continuum of a person's relationship with hope, moving from hopelessness, through skepticism, to being hopeful. The second (horizontal) axis he calls "Grasp of Reality," and its continuum describes how realistically a person sees a situation, moving from an uninformed, distorted, or denied reality, through to an informed, accurate, assimilated reality. The grid that is formed suggests four ways of relating to hope:

- helpless with no hope,
- wishful with false hope,
- surrendered with lost hope, or
- committed with real hope.[1]

My need for hope was intense, and I wouldn't let it go. Maybe I eschewed "helpless with no hope" because of my attachment to the fantasy that I could control the outcome of Tom's disease. I was unwilling to become "surrendered with no hope," wanting my refusal to yield to protect me from sinking into depression.

Much of my early hope fell into the category of "wishful with false hope." My innate optimistic worldview served me well, if only for a time. In the initial years, I felt that any hope, even false hope, would do. Yes, I had accurate information about dementia, but I had cordoned off that knowledge and restricted it to my head, not letting it seep into deeper heart-knowledge. Time and experience with dementia eventually forced me to accept the merciless disease process.

Acceptance of accurate reality caused me to revisit my hopes. In light of the inevitable, what could I hope for? Maybe more moments of clarity for Tom, however fleeting? Some moments of shared humor? A good night's sleep for him, and for me? I started to see that a good life is made up of small joys, not miracles. A specific hope might need to be relinquished, but another hope comes. Surrendering to reality does not mean the loss of all hope, it just means changed hope. This change is not loss or weakness. It is strength and flexibility.

Hope is a different thing for us dementia caregivers than it is for society at large. Besides having smaller hopes, we sometimes come to hope for things others might find objectionable. Maybe we hope that the disease process would hurry up, so our loved one could get beyond awareness of all the damage done to their brain. Maybe we hope our loved one's diabetes or heart disease would speed their death. Who is to judge such hopes? A good death with less suffering seems preferable to a protracted time in limbo.

One small research study[2] explored the experience of hope in dementia caregivers. The participants described their hope as the possibility of a positive future within both their daily lives and the limiting context of grief, loss, stress, and fatigue. False hope was carved away by experience, and hope was pared down to the real. The participants dealt with their fading hope by "renewing everyday hope," simple, ordinary, small hope. They did this through coming to terms with reality, seeking what was positive, and pursuing possibilities. Dementia caregivers learn to take hope in small doses, but we do take it.

The hope we carry probably doesn't look like the optimism that most people picture from Beaumont's category called "commitment with real hope." Our hope is not in temporal, quantitative, measurable reality but

in the reality we can't see. Henri Nouwen distinguishes between hope
and optimism from his Christian perspective:

> Hope has nothing to do with optimism. Many people think hope
> is optimism, looking at the positive side of life. But Jesus doesn't
> speak like that at all. . . . He describes wars, people in anguish,
> nation rising against nation. . . . There's no place that Jesus says,
> "One day it will all be wonderful." [He] says, "You need to pray
> unceasingly that you will keep your heart focused on me. Stand
> with your head erect."[3]

You may or may not want to focus on the person of Jesus, but you will
want to focus on your highest values. You will want to do that unceas-
ingly. When we stand erect doing that, we can look reality straight in the
eye and not cower.

Wisdom

"Hope" is the thing with feathers—
That perches in the soul—
And sings the tune without the words—
And never stops—at all—

And sweetest—in the Gale—is heard—
And sore must be the storm—
That could abash the little Bird
That kept so many warm—

I've heard it in the chillest land—
And on the strangest Sea—
Yet—never—in Extremity,
It asked a crumb—of me.

—Emily Dickinson[4]

If you live in hope, you can live very much in the present because you can nurture the footprints of God in your heart and life. . . . The whole of the spiritual life is saying that God is right with us, right now, so that we can wait for his coming, and this waiting is waiting in hope. . . . Here and now matter because God is a God of the present.

—Henri Nouwen[5]

Hope is an orientation of the spirit, an orientation of the heart; it transcends the world that is immediately experienced, and is anchored somewhere beyond its horizons. . . . It is not the conviction that something will turn out well, but the certainty that something makes sense, regardless of how it turns out. . . . [T]he deepest and most important form of hope, the only one that can keep us above water and urge us to good works . . . is something we get, as it were, from "elsewhere." It is also this hope, above all, which gives us the strength to live and continually to try new things, even in conditions that seem hopeless.

—Vaclav Havel[6]

For Your Consideration

- As a dementia caregiver, what is your experience of no hope? Of lost hope? Of false hope? Of real hope? In what ways has each kind of hope been helpful to you? Where has it tripped you up?
- If hope is different from wishing, for what would you wish? Consider those wishes in light of reality. What does it feel like to acknowledge reality?
- If you have had to surrender a false hope, what took its place?
- Has your "grasp of reality" changed during your time as a dementia caregiver? How? What caused that change?
- For what do you hope now? Does this, as Vaclav Havel suggests, give you strength?

Chapter Twenty-Two

• • • • • •

Intimacy

The last words Tom spoke to me came on a Valentine's Day. In a quiet alcove of the dining area in the care home, I had set a table for two, complete with a vase of fresh flowers and a lit candle. It was private, and we were unrushed. I fed him, one bite for him then one for me. Such a meal would be very strange for some, but for me it was intimate.

Afterward, I rolled Tom in his wheelchair to a nearby common room where we were alone. Holiday lights were still decorating the evergreen trees outside the windows, and their twinkling provided the only light we needed. I faced Tom, put one leg over his legs and half-stood, half-sat, straddling his legs. I leaned over and kissed his face, not once but many times. I unabashedly (for who cared but me?) kissed his ears and his nose and lips. Then he spoke his last words, "Like. Like."

Later, I took him to his room and gave him the care he needed before sleep—washing his face, combing his hair, brushing his teeth, transferring him via the Hoyer lift to the bed with the help of a nurse's aide, and putting up the bed's siderails. I got into the bed with him and I put my head on his once strong shoulder. Then I raised myself up on my elbow and kissed his lips. He did not—more accurately, could not—respond. I was neither wife nor widow.

116

Slowly I pried myself away from him, cutting the magnetism by sheer dint of will. As I left his room, I wondered as I had many times before if this would be our last goodbye or if it would become just the most recent one. Did he want to say, "I love you, Jean"? Who knows. But it pleased me to think so. Tom would always live in the deepest part of my heart, a place where no one else had been.

Reflections

Intimacy isn't only sexual. It is so much more. But sexual connection bespeaks the vulnerability that is required for intimacy. In intimacy, we are exposed to each other, meeting that deep need to be acknowledged and accepted.

If we have had intimacy with the person we care for, we grieve the profound loss of mutuality, of reciprocity. When two loving people are healthy, each holds up a mirror to the other so that they see themselves more clearly. When dementia sets in, we lose that mirror and the sweet communion of knowing and being known. We lose the one we trusted to speak truth to us. It's like part of ourselves is disappearing.

Losing mutual intimacy sometimes drives us to seek it elsewhere, maybe in some inappropriate places. My desire for intimacy drove me to thinking I was in love with someone I had only recently met. The poor man was the ambivalent recipient of my fantasies and projections. My advances were not reciprocated, which saved me from being mindlessly swallowed up in seeking short-term relief from a much deeper need. It was grace to have things go no further, to not seek such "a fragile shelter from a storming world," as Henri Nouwen describes such relationships. We could never have made it as a real couple in a real world.

Not everyone decides that extramarital intimacy is off-limits when dementia has taken away connection with their partner. A friend who is a dementia caregiver and also an ordained minister wrote to me confidentially at length, and said:

> If life—God—offers the gift of another person who says, "I love you"—perhaps born out of love for who you are as a caring

person, for what you do in your caring for another—there is no reason to hand back the gift, a precious gift, a life-restoring gift, to be relished by two people who have found each other in challenging circumstances. They can become deeply connected in love, love which has sexual overtones, because some touching is always present in love. But the erotic feelings may or may not be fully acted upon.

Of course, feelings of guilt may arise, prompted by judgment seen or imagined in the eyes of others; prompted too by self-judgment, by a sense of stretching or breaking a covenant. Then the two who have found themselves in love need to explore their understanding of God's love, asking, "Is it possible for someone to love two persons, when one of the beloveds is no longer capable of responding to love, while respecting and upholding the relationship between the cared for and the caregiver?"

People who value integrity and honesty do not say "yes" glibly; they can and do say "yes" from the voice of the heart and live joyfully in God's love and their human love.

Is there another kind of intimacy that can meet our deep need for touch and connection? I found it in the physical care I gave Tom. Cutting someone's hair and washing someone's feet may not sound like intimacy, but isn't it? When done with love and respect, do these acts not show deep affection and attachment? Do they not demonstrate trust and also vulnerability? It's not intellectual or emotional or sexual intimacy, but it is experiential intimacy.

There's another intimacy worth exploring, something I call Mother Bear intimacy. Mother bears are exceedingly protective of those in their care, and we become just that protective of our loved ones with dementia. We advocate for them within systems that too often fail to give them dignity. We demand that promises related to their care be honored, and we won't put up with excuses. Sometimes we are seen as ferocious, yet we don't blame mothers for protecting vulnerable young ones. Why then are we disparaging of those who are willing to go to the mat for their vulnerable loved ones who happen to be older and larger?

Of course, Mother Bear intimacy can be overdone and become smothering. It can squelch the dignity and independence of the person we care for. When caring for small children, overmothering can hurt a child because children learn from mistakes. But people with advanced dementia cannot learn, and mistakes made by them or to them can have devastating effects.

Taken too far, Mother Bear intimacy can be detrimental to the dementia caregiver too. Healthy boundaries between the caregiver and the care receiver can become so blurred that there is fusion of the two. Howard Gruetzner describes this: "Loved ones who have less of themselves must have more of [the caregiver]."[1] Taken to extreme, this kind of intimacy becomes a "bondage of symbiosis," where each needs the other in order to exist. It is no longer care of one by the other, but a complete blending of individuals.

The phrase "bondage of symbiosis" echoes "bonds of marriage" in my ears. Commitment and caregiving can be bondage, but can it not also reflect the depth of intimacy, or love? And is the caregiver to be blamed?

Wisdom

Unfortunately, as Alzheimer's Disease advances, it takes with it the personality, cognition, understanding, reasoning, and memories of our spouse. When they no longer possess the special characteristics with which we fell in love, how can our feelings not change? Passion and intimacy will eventually be replaced by the necessity for you to fulfill your spouse's personal hygiene needs—showering, dressing, and toileting. It is a brutally honest fact—the desire for sexual intimacy quickly dissipates in the face of changing adult diapers and cleaning the accompanying mess off of walls and floors.

—Joan Gershman[2]

I wonder if this is how people always get close: They heal each other's wounds; they repair the broken skin.

—Lauren Oliver[3]

A need, at times, to be together and talk,
And then the finding we can walk
More firmly through dark narrow places,
And meet more easily nightmare faces;
A need to reach out, sometimes, hand to hand,
And then find Earth less like an alien land;
A need for alliance to defeat
The whisperers at the corner of the street.

—A. S. J. Tessimond[4]

For Your Consideration

- How would you describe the kind of intimacy you formerly had with your loved one who now has dementia? How has that changed? Do you share any intimacy now?
- How do you handle the loss of mystery in your relationship? Have you lost that sense of specialness, or has it just changed?
- Do you sense that you have lost a trusted mirror being held for you by one who knows you deeply? How do you compensate for that?
- How do you handle your need for sexual, emotional, and intellectual intimacy?
- Do you crave touch? What are some ways you are or can be comfortably touched by another?
- Is there a memory you recall that makes the former intimacy alive even now?
- Have you experienced Mother Bear intimacy? If so, have you and your loved one been comfortable with that experience?

Chapter Twenty-Three

• • • • • •

Loneliness

In the middle phase of Tom's dementia, our physical selves were very together, "connected at the hip" as they say. It was the kind of togetherness that would be labeled unhealthy in a mature interdependent relationship, but our new relationship reflected Tom's growing dependence on me. Despite our physical closeness, our psyches and minds weren't able to connect as they had, making me and probably him experience a strange new loneliness. We were alone together. No one but Tom knew what we shared in our history, our secrets, our quirks, or our jokes. It felt as though part of my personal story was dying inside him.

The gift of his presence in my life had been so rare and precious. He could tell directions without a compass by looking at the moss on a tree trunk. He could start a fire with a bow drill. He could show me the shy orchid in the woods near the Tetons. He could read me poetry and he could complete my sentences. But that Tom had gone.

Friends tried to help. "You need to meet some new people," they advised. Meeting new people would take energy I didn't have. Besides, I didn't want new people—I wanted Tom! Who could ever fill his shoes? I didn't want company, no matter how kind or friendly. I wanted my partner back.

When Tom's dementia was quite advanced, some well-meaning friends would say, "He's not really there anymore, is he?" Those words brought little comfort and much irritation. Part of the old Tom was there, and I cherished being able to relate to his body, smelling the perspiration of his skin, massaging his now contracted fingers, even looking into his dulling blue eyes. He might no longer know I was his beloved wife, but he knew I was a caring person who stood by him.

Part, only part, of me was gone from him, just as only part of Tom was gone from me. We never intended it, but I think we both felt deserted, abandoned and alone.

Reflections

Loneliness is different from solitude. Solitude is enjoying your own company. Loneliness, like hunger, comes when you know what you are missing. In the ambiguous loss of loving someone with dementia, we have an ever-present reminder of what is missing. The misery is not a sharp pain, but an unremitting ache that shifts slightly when another skill is lost or a new behavior becomes troublesome.

Research on loneliness was a passion for John Cacioppo. He found, to no one's surprise, that loneliness is bad for your health. It has twice the impact on early death as obesity. It disrupts sleep, elevates blood pressure, and increases depression. Cacioppo also identified things that help ward off loneliness, what he describes as dimensions of healthy relationships.[1]

One of those dimensions is *collective connectedness*. This comes from feeling that we are part of something bigger than—and beyond—our small selves. Living in community can attach us to something bigger; so can belonging to a faith group, or participating in a social action group. Yet dementia caregivers don't have much discretionary time to join new groups; we hardly have time to give to groups of which we are already a part. We can, however, remind others in our groups that we still exist and still care. If we are lucky, that might spark them to reach out to us in our growing isolation.

Another dimension of healthy affiliation is *relational connectedness*. This involves contacts that are face-to-face and mutually rewarding.

Having coffee with someone on a regular basis, attending a support group—these can help meet that need even when family and old friends are no longer nearby. Interacting with others makes us more interesting and brings the outside world into one that has become confined.

Friendship is a precious kind of relational connectedness. Ann Lewin is a poet and dementia caregiver who warns, "Friendships don't always survive a period of non-availability."[2] Caregivers are overcommitted and often unavailable. But it's not just our nonavailability. Some friends leave us. Some pull away because they feel uncomfortable with the changes brought by dementia. Some couples withdraw because the old foursome is no longer. Losing friends compounds our loneliness, but thank goodness other friends are willing to witness our loss and sadness. Doing so, they teach us how precious friendship is. We come to value these friends all the more. Dementia has taught us that relationships are delicate and that none can last forever. Good friends ought never be taken for granted.

Cacioppo's third dimension is *intimate connectedness*. It comes from having someone in your life who affirms you for who you are. This level of connection is most profound, and losing it is devastating. With dementia, we lose one who (as the Sufis say) "polished our souls" by rubbing off our rough edges, loving us in the process.

So how is one to find intimate connection? The short answer is "With great patience and enough time," and we may be short on both. Deep connection cannot be hurried no matter how great the loneliness. Intimate connection can only be nurtured as we nurture any friendship: spending time together, exchanging ideas, being gentle with each other, not forcing ourselves on each other, and sharing vulnerabilities. With experience, trust develops.

Many years ago when I lost a very important relationship, my sister suggested I write a list of ten things I enjoy having friends do for me. My list included bringing me their copy of the *Sunday Times* after they had finished reading it and bringing me flowers. She said, "Now do those things for yourself. Buy yourself flowers. Become your own best friend." A deeper friendship with myself developed as I knew myself better, becoming more tender with my shortcomings, feeling my feelings instead of burying them, and noticing what my body was telling me.

If only we could see ourselves as a loving God might see us and delight in us. Maybe loneliness is telling us that we need a deeper friendship with God as well as with ourselves. Psychologists might call this sublimation, diverting the energy from one purpose to another. If it is a defense mechanism, is that so bad? True, it has none of the saltiness of human intimate connection, but it is a way out of loneliness and into solitude.

Through the centuries, people have found a relationship with God to be profoundly comforting and freeing. Developing this connection is done the way any relationship is nurtured. The venue might be different from human connection, but the actions are similar: spending time together, paying attention, being honest, opening to joy and pain, developing trust.

Friends who can't be physically present to each other often have mementos around that help them to remember the other—a picture, a note, a poem. They bring the unseen into view. Religious or spiritual artifacts can do that too.

Loneliness can slowly morph into solitude. In my solitude, I began to apprehend that God was with me, inside me, and was present no matter where I was, or who I was with, or what I was feeling. I also realized that the very best of Tom was in me and that wouldn't leave.

Wisdom

Rejoice, and men will seek you;
Grieve, and they turn and go;
They want full measure of all your pleasure,
But they do not need your woe.
Be glad, and your friends are many;
Be sad, and you lose them all,—
There are none to decline your nectared wine,
But alone you must drink life's gall.

—Ella Wheeler Wilcox[3]

There is nothing that can replace the absence of someone dear to us, and one should not even attempt to do so. One must simply hold out and endure it. At first that sounds very hard, but at the same time it is also a great comfort. For to the extent the emptiness truly remains unfilled one remains connected to the other person through it. . . . Gratitude transforms the torment of memory into silent joy. One bears what was lovely in the past not as a thorn but as a precious gift deep within, a hidden treasure of which one can always be certain.

—Dietrich Bonhoeffer[4]

Loneliness is the poverty of self; solitude is richness of self.

—May Sarton[5]

The big and hidden secret is this: an infinite God seeks and desires intimacy with the human soul. Once you experience such intimacy, only the intimate language of lovers describes what is going on for you: mystery, tenderness, singularity, specialness, changing the rules "for me," nakedness, risk, ecstasy, incessant longing, and of course also, necessary suffering.

—Richard Rohr[6]

For Your Consideration

- Try making a diagram to illustrate who you are connected with now. What does this tell you about your ability to connect? How does this inform your loneliness?
- Identify ten things that you enjoy having others do for you. Is it possible that you can do these for yourself?
- Do you sense that you are part of anything bigger than yourself? How does that connection touch your sense of loneliness?
- Can you imagine caring for your loneliness like a friend would care for you, with sensitivity and kindness? What might that compassion feel like?

- Have you tried to replace the lost connection you once had with your loved one who has dementia? How has that worked out?
- Would you say that the relationship you had with your loved one is worth the pain you experience in losing that connection? Do you experience any of the "silent joy" of which Bonhoeffer speaks?
- If you have moved from loneliness to experiencing solitude, does God meet you in your solitude? Do you relate to the words of Richard Rohr about intimacy with God? Can you sense that relationship filling you up inside?

Chapter Twenty-Four

• • • • • •

Resentment

I am not proud of my resentments, but they were a real part of my experience in dementia caregiving. Maybe this is time for my true confessions. Maybe some of this will resonate with you.

I resented the systems that gave only lip service to valuing the care I gave. I was one of 11,200,000 dementia caregivers giving, each year, 15,300,000,000 hours of unpaid care that was valued at $257,700,000,000.¹ In exchange, not one of us who worked so hard earned any credit toward our Social Security benefits. We received no medical insurance, at least not until we impoverished ourselves enough to be eligible for Medicaid. Besides not getting paid for my labor, it cost me financially as I dipped into retirement savings, refused promotion, and cut to part-time work and part-pay. Obviously, I did the caring because of my relationship with Tom, but I also did it for a society that says it cares for its citizens. I resented being taken for granted.

I'm ashamed to say I also started to resent family, though they did no wrong. I could understand their level of assistance: no one lived nearby; they had other obligations; they had their own fears and reasons for not wanting to see dementia close up; they might feel embarrassed giving care to Tom. They were busy marrying, retiring, moving, taking new jobs, and birthing babies. All that made sense. But it still left me alone giving the care. While I had diminishing reserves of cash and energy, I pictured our children and siblings going about their busy, distant lives, far from Tom's wandering and neediness.

To be fair, my request for someone to stay with Tom when my work took me out of town was often honored. For that I am deeply grateful. Yet no one suggested moving closer to Tom in order to offer more support, and no one invited us to move closer to them so they could help. I thought, "If I were not caring for their father/brother, who would be? Were not their careers and paychecks intact, while mine were not? Was I not giving an enormous gift to them, as well as gifting Tom?"

I sent e-mails to family members, telling them how Tom was doing. Their responses were always sincere and they thanked me, writing, "We are so grateful that you are taking such good care of him. We trust you. Do what you think is best." They gave me permission to make decisions and use my best judgment. While I appreciated their confidence, I was left with the weight of responsibility squarely on my shoulders, and my shoulders were tired.

Reflections

Resentment happens when a person feels offended for being treated unfairly. It's a perception, not an objective reality. It's also insidious and can be dangerous.

We try to keep our resentments to ourselves, reasoning that they are small, shameful, and best kept hidden, but they are not kept inside. They show on our faces with gritted teeth and clenched jaws. They show in our touchiness, and they appear in our sarcasm. We think we are hiding them under a forced smile, but the message that we are displeased still comes across. Our communication becomes ambiguous at best. Embarrassed by our resentment, we have trouble speaking our truth and become less and less self-disclosing. That gnaws at our hearts. We start to feel like victims. Eventually, resentment holds us prisoner, depriving us of serenity as it smolders.

Dementia, like any other crisis in a family, brings to the fore a family's dynamics, the habitual ways family members interact. The dynamics have long been there, probably not in our consciousness but just below the horizon. The tendency of the family either to circle the wagons when faced with crisis or to pull away from each other becomes apparent. Dyad alliances become stronger. The take-charge person takes charge, and the silent one withdraws. The traditional roles of peacemaker and scapegoat are enacted. We ought not be surprised when family dynamics become more pronounced, but we always are. It would help to step back and recognize them, not to judge them as right-or-wrong, good-or-bad, but just as reality. It's a chance to say, "Here we are, doing what we do." This may not be the time to attempt changing the dynamics, but it is time to notice them and take them for what they are.

Resentment offers us a false air of righteousness, a tenuous means of clinging to self-respect. The next step beyond such resentment is to become a martyr. From there, feeling more and more alone, we put even more effort into giving care and overfunctioning, trying to prove our value and goodness to the world. The cycle continues in a downward spiral.

Is there a good way to handle feelings of resentment? David Mass says resentment is carrying "excess weight that needs to be shed," like carrying around tumors that are accepted as part of ourselves rather than as hideous, life-threatening growths.[2] But how do we find the strength to do that shedding? It starts with looking inside at the source of the resentments.

Resentment occurs when we betray ourselves on behalf of another and then blame them. Betraying ourselves is second nature for those of us raised to value putting the needs of others ahead of our own needs. Sadly, as we adopt this seemingly generous habit, we are disobeying the wisdom of so many spiritual teachers: Love your neighbor *as* you love yourself, not *instead* of yourself. If we don't honor and love (and I don't mean indulge) ourselves, how can we freely honor and love another?

Righting the wrong of self-betrayal means taking the initiative to express ourselves and to honor our feelings. That done, options expand and we can ask new questions: How can we care for ourselves as well as the one we love? How do we best address the absence of help and then ask for assistance? We do have the power to change the situation, not by changing the behavior of others, but by stopping the betrayal of our God-given selves.

Donald Hicks wisely says, "At the heart of all anger, all grudges, and all resentment, you'll find a fear that hopes to stay anonymous."[3] Don't let that happen. Look deeply, carefully, and lovingly at what it is that you fear. Don't let it be anonymous. Name it. Maybe it's fear of complete exhaustion, or of ruining your own health, or losing your identity as anyone besides a dementia caregiver. Take the time you need to pay attention to what's inside you, underneath the resentment. Stand in that pain and own it. It will not kill you, and it will strengthen you, because you are claiming responsibility for your own life.

Maybe then you will find ways to express your fear to the person you resent without accusation or belittling. Maybe together you can find a way forward. The plan won't be perfect and will require compromise, but it will be good enough to free you from resentment because you will have spoken your truth.

No one can read your mind to discover your needs, and no one else knows what you are going through, no matter how obvious you think it is. It might be a new experience to specifically ask for what you need. Rather than leaving the open-ended offer of help ("Let me know if I can ever do anything") to just flap in the breeze say, "Yes, you can help by. . . ." Be specific about what you need. Keep a running list. What's the worst that can happen? That they will say no? Would you be any worse off?

Speaking of *no*, your *no* might need to be exercised a bit more. "No, I can't give her care for a whole week without a day to recuperate and recharge." "No, I can't pay for that equipment. Maybe you can?" Remember that the more you take on, the more you will be asked to take on. What you allow in terms of interpersonal dynamics will continue. Saying *no* and standing your ground is not self-effacing and may not meet some cultural expectation, but being nice is hardly the point under the challenging circumstances you face every single day. Being clear is not being mean.

There is something you can do that is nice, though. Imagine what the person to whom you bear resentment is experiencing. Mentally, walk in their shoes for a few miles to get a sense of their experience. See if you have a change of attitude. I did. Tom's children no doubt had grave fear that they too would develop dementia and didn't want to see it. His siblings were likely hesitant to step on my toes or to question my decisions, for I would have been a formidable opponent. A bit of empathy helps.

There is nothing fair about dementia. Don't make it worse by taking offense.

Wisdom

The older brother became angry and refused to go in [to the party]. So his father went out and pleaded with him. But he answered his father, "Look! All these years I've been slaving for you and never disobeyed your orders. Yet you never gave me even a young goat so I could celebrate with my friends. But when this son of yours who has squandered your property with prostitutes comes home, you kill the fattened calf for him!" "My son," the father said, "you are always with me, and everything I have is yours."

—Luke 15:28–31, NIV

Comparisons always leave us in a bad place. We either judge ourselves better than someone, which is the toxin of pride; or we judge ourselves worse than someone else, which tarnishes our own dignity and may affect theirs. God gives each one of us a story line, and our story is our story, like none other.

—Curtis Almquist[4]

Keep a sharp eye out for weeds of bitter discontent. A thistle or two gone to seed can ruin a whole garden in no time.

—Hebrews 12:14–16, *The Message*

For Your Consideration

- Have you felt used or taken for granted as a dementia caregiver? What was that like?
- Have you been on the receiving end of resentment? How did you know you were resented? How did that feel?

- Sometimes resentment, like anger, gives us energy and spurs us forward to change. Have you had that experience? Describe it.
- How does carrying resentment impact your dementia caregiving?
- Is there anything you have done or are doing that feeds your feelings of resentment?
- Can you identify some actions or attitudes you can engage in to help you become more free of resentment?
- If there is person you resent now, imagine yourself as that person and fill in the blanks of these sentences using their voice: "My deepest longing for the person in my life who has dementia is. . . . My deepest longing for myself is. . . . My deepest fear is. . . ." Reflect on what you imagine their answers to be. Do you feel any differently toward this person?

Chapter Twenty-Five

• • • • • •

Thankfulness

Three years before Tom died, I wrote this in my journal: "I shed tears of thankfulness for the first time in ages." My jottings reminded me that on that evening in early November, Tom was actually happy when I took him back to the care home, and he offered no resistance. We had been visiting old friends at their home, and he had laughed and gorged on carry-out pizza.

That breakthrough sparked my awareness of other gifts that I had received from dementia caregiving, like the gift of my own growth, the stretching and developing of parts of myself I hadn't known were there. I was thankful for the gift of Tom's presence in my life and that he had changed me for the better. I was grateful that I could say "Thank you" to Tom, and seal it with a kiss. Till the moment he died, I was thankful I could touch him.

At our wedding so many years earlier, we sang a hymn by Jaroslav Vajda. It was written with no punctuation and with sixteen repetitions of the word *now*.[1] During the dementia years of our marriage, we learned we actually *had* to live in the now. Living with eyes wide open, we credited that "nowness" with the joy we were able to savor. I was thankful for Tom's willingness and ability to shed tears and face squarely his impending diminishments. Our last year together was

peppered with my sometimes tearful outbursts of, "Thank you, Tom!"
I even found myself thankful that I was going through this ordeal of
dementia with him, hoping that I might emerge as a more compassionate person. In those moments of gratitude, the joy of our relationship
outweighed the pain.

Milton Mayerhoff says, "Gratitude is a natural expression of being
in-place."[2] Living in the fullness of the now, Tom and I were truly in-
place, honestly being who we were and allowing our lives to unfold as
they would. When I was younger, I was grateful for the things that
brought me ease and pleasure, and I would deplore the things that were
uncomfortable. Growing older has taught me that there is gift in the
dark things of life, and if I am patient, I can welcome them too as inte-
gral to the fullness and completeness of life.

If you call me Pollyanna, you wouldn't be the first. Truth be told, I'd
rather be grateful than bitter.

Reflections

The old adage says that it is not happy people who are thankful; it is
thankful people who are happy. Happiness doesn't come as a result
of getting something we didn't have, but rather from recognizing and
appreciating what we do have. We are wise to want what we have, if not
constantly, at least regularly. Simply taking enough interest to notice
what we have is the beginning of that happiness. The process of paying
attention and finding gifts starts slowly, but it's worth every effort.

Gratitude isn't a quick or casual thank-you. It's much deeper. It's a
conscious choice, maybe even a discipline. One can choose to be grateful, even while other feelings, like hurt or sadness, exist simultaneously.
We cheat ourselves when we reserve gratitude for the parts of our experience that we like, natural as that might seem initially. If we divide our
thoughts and memories into the categories of either good or bad, our
lives are depleted. Henri Nouwen tells us that such thinking "prevents us
from truly allowing our whole past to be the source from which we live
our future. . . . When our gratitude for the past is only partial, our hope
for a new future can never be full."[3] Our lives are all of one piece. You've

heard, "Shit happens." Well, compost happens too. Maybe there is truth in the popular maxim "It's all good."

Gratefulness is a reminder that we do not walk this Earth as independent entities, but as people who need others. Dementia caregivers certainly learn this as we depend on so many people and face a myriad of factors over which we have no control. Some might see this reliance as degrading. Others find it humbling and liberating. Nouwen writes:

> When a man is able to thank, he is able to know his limitations without feeling defensive and to be self-confident without being proud. He claims his own powers and at the same time he confesses his need for help. Thanking in a real sense avoids submissiveness as well as possessiveness. It is the act of a free man who can say: I thank you.[4]

Sometimes we receive gifts from people we've never even met. Sometimes we receive gifts that we didn't even know we needed. Maybe that's when we need to simply thank God.

Wisdom

Who does not thank for little will not thank for much.

—Estonian proverb

Life is this simple: we are living in a world that is absolutely transparent and God is shining through it all the time. . . . If we abandon ourselves to God and forget ourselves, we see it sometimes and we see it maybe frequently. . . . It becomes very obvious that God is everywhere and in every thing, and we cannot be without [God]. It is impossible. The only thing is that we don't see it.

—Thomas Merton[5]

In the midst of this pain, there is a strange, shocking, yet very surprising voice. It is the voice of the one who says: "Blessed are those who mourn; they shall be comforted." That's the unexpected news: there is a blessing hidden in our grief. Somehow, in the midst of our mourning, the first steps of the dance take place. Somehow, the cries that well up from our losses belong to the songs of gratitude.

—Henri Nouwen[6]

One regret, dear world,
That I am determined not to have
When I am lying on my deathbed
Is that
I did not kiss you enough.

—Hafiz[7]

For Your Consideration

- Have you experienced being grateful and needy at the same time? What was that like?
- Name at least ten things for which you are thankful now. They can be attitudes, gifts, experiences, relationships—anything at all. Do you find any surprises?
- How do you understand the value of thankfulness?
- How do you feel in both body and soul when you are thankful?
- What has gratitude meant in your life?

Part Five

"Are We There Yet?"

Chapter Twenty-Six

• • • • • •

Home

When Tom was in the first care home, he often said he wanted to go home. I was very unsure of what his response would be to seeing our house, yet I needed to take the risk. One warm Sunday afternoon, I drove to the care home, picked him up, and took him to get ice cream. Still dithering, I drove him to our home. We pulled partway into the driveway and stopped, looking at the building for a while from the inside of the car. "Would you like to go inside?" I asked. His reply was clear, both from the fear on his face and the shaking of his head; it was a resounding "No!"

Slowly I realized what was happening. This place was not what Tom meant when he said home. Maybe home was his childhood home in Newton, Massachusetts, with the safety of his parents. Despite having lived in our low-slung, midcentury house for seventeen years, it was foreign to him, just like the care home was foreign, just like every place was foreign.

Home had a different meaning to each of us. We were truly walking each other home, but the expected destinations were different. I was accompanying him to his home beyond mortal life and I was going elsewhere, at least for a while, to a new life right here on Earth. But where was that new life, that new home? I wanted this dementia nightmare to be over. I wanted to awaken to a bright day full of possibility. I just didn't know where to find it, or if it even existed.

Honoring the hope of coming to the end of the long journey as a dementia caregiver, I bought myself a small gold ring. I wore it on the fourth finger of my right hand, balancing the wedding band on my left hand. It was a reminder to myself that just as I was committed to Tom in marriage, I was committed to my own life as well, to caring for myself both now and after Tom left his vale of tears.

I'm not sure just what I was expecting of life after Tom's death. I had coveted the freedom, yet I hadn't pictured what it would look like. Instead of being a new vista, it was a vacuum. Tom's last breath was a watershed moment, despite its being long anticipated. Suddenly I had no one to cradle or advocate for. Having come to the deep yet narrow place of dementia caregiving, I found that the wider world didn't notice or give a care about my well-honed skills. The health care system no longer needed me to be Tom's primary caregiver. The rest of the family didn't need me to be the go-to person. Tom certainly no longer needed my care. Exhausted, I was not about to jump into another caregiving situation. I was useless, having been so very useful for thirteen years. I was lost in a strange new world.

Both gold rings were on my fingers for several months after Tom's death. A friend asked me when I'd be taking off the wedding ring and gave me a tip: using Windex helps rings slide off easily. Curious, when next I was cleaning house, I casually tried it. Amazed, and a bit shocked, the ring slipped from the place that had kept it (and my heart) safe for two decades.

Reflections

Having faithfully walked our loved ones to their dying and their home beyond this earthly life, do *we* arrive at home? Can we relax and let down our guard? Can we get on with living as widows and widowers and orphans?

After the initial shock waves of death, we begin to take stock of our lives. We find we have been cast into a world that has gone on without our involvement. It is neither the world we left nor the world we imagined. We discover how constricted our lives had become. We find that the new dementia-free future is just as nebulous as the dementia-driven past. It's not the familiar old home, but a new one, a place where we need to learn the noises of the house, discover the quirks of the heating and plumbing, meet the neighbors, and plant a garden in unfamiliar soil. Understandably, we feel a bit shaky, and maybe skeptical.

Coming into this new world is like being birthed all over again. And birth is no easy matter. An infant inside her mother's womb—cramped and predictable as that prebirth life is—knows only that constricted world and nothing of the larger world or new life. The baby doesn't know what she will have to endure: being massaged and then pushed and shoved by her mother's contractions and squeezed through a narrow birth canal. Once pressured into the life of the outside world, she meets cold air and unfamiliar touch for the first time. She learns to breathe, no longer able to passively exist on the reliable nourishment and oxygen brought by the umbilical cord. She experiences hunger for the first time. Exhausted, she needs sleep. Rested, she begins to explore things she couldn't have imagined inside the womb: colors, textures, smells, sounds, movements, tastes. All new. All glorious and begging to be explored.

Dementia caregivers are also birthed into new life, and though it is a new life, it has a profound connection to our old one. Ram Dass reminds us that "wherever we go, there we are." It's quite like a caterpillar morphing into a butterfly: its life has the very same DNA throughout its experience of noshing on leaves, enclosing in a chrysalis, melting into a deranged soup, and being reassembled into a thing with wings. Our DNA hasn't changed either. We become a new version of ourselves. Through spiritual alchemy, we find ourselves transfigured, the same and yet different. We have had a metamorphosis, a changing of form. We didn't seek the change any more than the poor caterpillar did, but we do find we are more completely ourselves. We won't—and can't—throw away the past. We can never unknow what we now know, nor would we want to dispose of what the long, hard journey has taught us. Hopefully we are not embittered but have become people with a greater and more mature love for ourselves, for life, and the whole wide world.

In the fourteenth century, Julian of Norwich moved into a most uncommon new home. As an anchoress, she chose to live her life in the confines of one room attached to a church building. From that very limited place, she offers us this consolation, easing our transition. Holding a small hazelnut in the palm of her hand, she sees in it life. She marvels:

> I thought that [the hazelnut] might fall into nothing for little-ness. . . . In this little thing I saw three properties. The first is that God made it. The second that God loves it. And the third that God keeps it. God did not say, "Thou shalt not be tempested, thou shalt not be travailed, thou shalt not be dis-eased," but God said, "Thou shalt not be overcome. . . . All shall be well, and all shall be well, and all manner of thing shall be well."[1]

Wisdom

A disciple asks the rebbe: "Why does Torah tell us to 'place these words upon your hearts'? Why does it not tell us to place these holy words *in* our hearts?" The rebbe answers: "It is because as we are, our hearts are closed, and we cannot place the holy words in our hearts. So we place them on top of our hearts. And there they stay until, one day, the heart breaks and the words fall in."

—Hasidic tale[2]

The time will come
when, with elation
you will greet yourself arriving
at your own door, in your own mirror
and each will smile at the other's welcome,

and say, sit here. Eat.
You will love again the stranger who was your self.
Give wine. Give bread. Give back your heart
to itself, to the stranger who has loved you

all your life, whom you ignored
for another, who knows you by heart.
Take down the love letters from the bookshelf,

the photographs, the desperate notes,
peel your own image from the mirror.
Sit. Feast on your life.

—Derek Walcott[3]

For Your Consideration

- What does *home* mean to you? What do you suppose it has meant to your loved one with dementia?
- Is it possible to be both on the journey and at home simultaneously? If so, how does that work?
- What might it be like to travel alone, having been left by the loved one who has accompanied you on this journey? How will you know that you are home?
- What difficulties do you foresee in embracing your new life? What are the blessings you anticipate? Do you have a sense that you will be able to do as Walcott invites, to "feast on your life"?

Afterword

Western society is still trying to sell us on a false definition of success. We're told "Get more, do more, be more, and thus you will find success and happiness." But having taken the long journey of dementia caregiving, we know that success is something quite different. We know that all the money and power in the world cannot keep our loved ones healthy or keep our hearts from breaking open. We know that, in the end, all that matters is Love.

John of the Cross said, "In the evening, we shall be examined on love." The contemporary poet Thomas Centolella elaborates on those words. I offer them to you in closing.

"In the evening, we shall be examined on love."
And it won't be multiple choice,
though some of us would prefer it that way.
Neither will it be essay, which tempts us to run on
when we should be sticking to the point, if not together.
In the evening there shall be implications
our fear will change to complications. No cheating,
we'll be told, and we'll try to figure the cost of being true
to ourselves. In the evening when the sky has turned
that certain blue, blue of exam books, blue of no more
daily evasions, we shall climb the hill as the light empties
and park our tired bodies on a bench above the city
and try to fill in the blanks. And we won't be tested
like defendants on trial, cross-examined
till one of us breaks down, guilty as charged. No,
in the evening, after the day has refused to testify,
we shall be examined on love like students

who don't even recall signing up for the course
and now must take their orals, forced to speak for once
from the heart and not off the top of their heads.
And when the evening is over and it's late,
the student body asleep, even the great teachers
retired for the night, we shall stay up
and run back over the questions, each in our own way:
what's true, what's false, what unknown quantity
will balance the equation, what it would mean years from now
to look back and know
we did not fail.[1]

Notes

Introduction

1. There are many versions of this tale. A similar one (along with many stories) can be found in *Classic Tales of Mulla Nasreddin*, retold by Houman Farzad, translated from Persian by Diane L. Wilcox (Costa Mesa, CA, Mazda Publishers, 1989), 26.
2. Maya Angelou, "Human Family," in *I Shall Not Be Moved* (repr.; New York: Bantam, 1991), 4.

Chapter 1

1. Antonio Machado, *There Is No Road*, trans. by Mary Berg and Dennis Maloney (Buffalo, NY: White Pine Press, 2003), 55. Used by permission.
2. Chuck Palahniuk, *Survivor* (New York: W. W. Norton, 2010).
3. Abhijit Naskar, *Monk Meets World* (N.p., 2019). Accessed at https://www.goodreads.com/quotes/tag/without-direction.
4. John O'Donohue, "For a New Beginning," in *To Bless the Space between Us: A Book of Blessings* (New York: Doubleday, 2008), 14. Used by permission.

Chapter 2

1. Stephan G. Weit, "Top 4 Caregiver Needs," ElderCaring (blog), September 10, 2009, https://checkincalls.wordpress.com/2009/09/10/top-4-caregiver-needs.
2. John W. Travis and Regina Sara Ryan, *Wellness Workbook*, 3rd ed. (Berkeley: Celestial Arts, 2004), xxi.
3. Attributed to Lou Holtz, former football player. Accessed at https://www.goodreads.com/quotes/search?utf8=%E2%9C%93&q=Lou+Holtz&commit=Search
4. Brené Brown, *The Gifts of Imperfection* (Center City, MN: Hazelden Publishing, 2010).

Chapter 3

1. Peta Bowden, *Caring: Gender Sensitive Ethics* (London: Routledge, 1997), 183.
2. Joan C. Tronto, *Moral Boundaries: A Political Argument for an Ethic of Care* (New York: Routledge, 1994), 106–8.
3. Rosalynn Carter, *Helping Yourself Help Others: A Book for Caregivers* (New York: Three Rivers Press, 1994).
4. Alzheimer's Association, "2021 Alzheimer's Disease Facts and Figures," https://www.alz.org/media/Documents/alzheimers-facts-and-figures.pdf.
5. Sheila Neysmith, quoted in Howard Gruetzner, *Alzheimer's: The Complete Guide for Families and Loved Ones*, 2nd ed. (New York: John Wiley and Sons, 1997), 183.
6. Tronto, *Moral Boundaries*, 111.
7. Alistair Campbell, *Moderated Love: A Theology of Professional Care* (London: Society for Promoting Christian Knowledge, 1984), 106.
8. Milton Mayerhoff, *On Caring* (New York: Perennial Library, 1971), 21.

Chapter 4

1. Wendell Berry, "Section X of Sabbaths, 1998," in *Given* (Washington DC: Shoemaker Hoard, 2005), 65–66. Permission granted through personal communication.
2. Walt Whitman, "Song of the Open Road," Poetry Foundation, accessed May 19, 2021, https://www.poetryfoundation.org/poems/48859/song-of-the-open-road. Public domain.

Chapter 5

1. Alzheimer's Association, "2021 Alzheimer's Disease Facts and Figures," https://www.alz.org/media/Documents/alzheimers-facts-and-figures.pdf.
2. Marilyn Geewax. "Discovering the True Cost of At-Home Caregiving," *Family Matters: The Money Squeeze*, NPR, May 1, 2012, https://www.npr.org/2012/05/01/151472617/discovering-the-true-cost-of-at-home-caregiving.
3. Alzheimer's Association, "2019 Alzheimer's Disease Facts and Figures," https://www.alz.org/media/documents/alzheimers-facts-and-figures-2019-r.pdf.
4. Alzheimer's Association, "2021 Alzheimer's Disease Facts and Figures."
5. Suzanne M. Cahill, "Caring in Families: What Motivates Wives, Daughters, and Daughters-in-law to Provide Dementia Care?" *Journal of Family Studies* 5, no. 2 (December 7, 2014): 235–47, https://doi.org/10.5172/jfs.5.2.235.
6. Carol J. Farran, "Theoretical Perspectives Concerning Positive Aspects of Caring for Elderly Persons with Dementia: Stress/Adaptation and

Existentialism," *The Gerontologist* 37, no. 2 (April 1, 1997): 250–57, https://doi.org/10.1093/geront/37.2.250.

7. Catherine Quinn, Linda Clare, and Robert T. Woods, "The Impact of Motivations and Meanings on the Wellbeing of Caregivers of People with Dementia: A Systematic Review," *International Psychogeriatrics* 22, no. 1 (February 2010): 43–55, https://doi.org/10.1017/S1041610209990810.

8. Whitman, "Song of the Open Road." Public domain.

9. Wendell Berry, *Another Turn of the Crank*, as quoted in *The Sacred Earth: Writers on Nature and Spirit*, ed. Jason Gardner (Novato, CA: New World Library, 1998), 115. Here, Berry is talking about environmental issues and his use of "creatures" refers to other animals. I believe it applies to human creatures too.

10. Nicholas Berdyaev, "The Destiny of Man," as quoted by Martin L Smith in *A Season for the Spirit* (Cambridge, MA: Cowley Publications, 1991), 61.

Chapter 6

1. Richard Rohr, *Eager to Love: The Alternative Way of Francis of Assisi* (Cincinnati, OH: Franciscan Media, 2016), especially 183–87.

2. Rudolf Otto, *The Idea of the Holy*, 2nd ed., trans. John W. Harvey (Oxford: Oxford University Press, 1950).

3. R. S. Thomas, "Tell Us," in *Collected Later Poems: 1988–2000* (Northumberland, UK: Bloodaxe Books, 2004), 170. Used by permission.

4. Fredrick Faber, "There's a wideness in God's mercy," Hymn #461 in *The New English Hymnal* (Norwich, UK: Canterbury Press, 1986). Public domain.

5. Hafiz, "We Should Talk About This Problem," in Daniel Ladinsky, *I Heard God Laughing* (New York: Penguin Books, 2006), 4. Used by permission.

6. Rumi, "Let's Go Home," in John Moyne and Coleman Barks, *Open Secret: Versions of Rumi* (Putney, VT: Threshold Books, 1984), 55. Used by permission.

Chapter 7

1. James Montgomery, quoted in Robert Carruthers, "The Poetical Works of James Montgomery: With a Memoir" (1858). Public domain.

2. Ralph Martin, *Fulfilment of All Desire* (Steubenville, OH: Emmaus Road Publishing, 2006), 121.

3. *The Book of Common Prayer* (New York: Church Publishing, 1979), 856.

4. Pierre Teilhard de Chardin, quoted in Robert J. Furey, *The Joy of Kindness* (Spring Valley, NY: Crossroad Publishing, 1930), 138.

5. "Eternal Spirit of the Living Christ." Words by Frank von Christierson © 1974 The Hymn Society (Admin. Hope Publishing Company, Carol Stream, IL 60188). All rights reserved. Used by permission

6. Ann Lewin, "Disclosure," in *Watching for the Kingfisher: Poems and Prayers* (Norwich, UK: Canterbury Press, 2009), 31. Used by permission.

7. Rumi, quoted in Allahbakhsh Brohi, "The Spiritual Dimension of Prayer," in *Islamic Spirituality: Foundations*, ed. Seyyed Hossein Nasr (London: SCM Press, 1989), 136.

Chapter 8

1. The excellent website developed by Mary Ann and Frederic Brussat can be enjoyed at www.spiritualityandpractice.org.

2. You can locate a spiritual director by going to https://www.sdicompanions .org/find-a-spiritual-director-companion/.

3. I heard him make this statement in a lecture he gave at Christ Church, Ontario, California, winter 2019.

4. Abraham Joshua Herschel, *I Asked for Wonder: A Spiritual Anthology*, ed. Samuel H. Dresner (New York: Crossroad, 1995), 65.

Chapter 9

1. "For Quiet Confidence," *The Book of Common Prayer* (New York: Church Publishing, 1979), 832.

2. Yehuda Amichai, "A Man in His Life," in *Selected Poetry of Yehuda Amichai* (Literature of the Middle East), trans. Chana Bloch and Stephen Mitchell (Oakland, CA: University of California Press, 1996).

3. Robert J. Johnson, *Owning Your Own Shadow*, rep. ed. (New York: HarperCollins, 2013), 107.

4. John Wesley, "A Catholic Spirit," The Voice, Christian Resource Institute, 2018, http://www.crivoice.org/cathspirit.html. This sermon has been edited into more modern English from the 1872 reprint of the 1771 edition of John Wesley's *Fifty-Three Sermons*.

5. Rumi, "The Guest House," in *Selected Poems by Rumi*, trans. Coleman Barks (London: Penguin Classics, 2004),109. Used by permission.

6. Henri Nouwen, *Bread for the Journey* (San Francisco: HarperOne, 1996), 123.

Chapter 10

1. https://www.goodreads.com/quotes/3234701-there-exists-only-the-present -instant-a-now-which-always.

2. Joseph Stein, "Fiddler on the Roof," quoted in *The Best of Sholem Aleichem*, ed. Irving Howe et al. (Washington, DC: New Republic Books, 1979).

3. Curtis Almquist, "Investing in Life—Br. Curtis Almquist," Society of Saint John the Evangelist, November 16, 2008, http://ssje.org/ssje/2008/11/16 /investing-in-life.

4. Joan Chittister, *The Gift of Years* (New York: BlueBridge, 2010), 61.

5. Henri Nouwen, *Can You Drink the Cup?* (Notre Dame, IN: Ave Maria Press, 1996), 81–82.

Chapter 11

1. Carol Tavris, *Anger: The Misunderstood Emotion* (New York: Simon and Schuster, 1982), 96.
2. George Herbert, "The Church Porch," in *The Temple, The Country Parson.* (London: Society for Promoting Christian Knowledge, 1981), 132.
3. Thich Nhat Hahn, *Anger: Buddhist Wisdom for Cooling the Flames* (New York: Riverhead Books, 2001).
4. C. FitzSimons Allison, *Guilt, Anger, and God: The Patterns of our Discontent* (New York: Seabury Press, 1972), 29.
5. Alastair Campbell, *The Gospel of Anger* (London: Society for Promoting Christian Knowledge, 1983), 14.
6. Allison, *Guilt, Anger, and God*, 7.
7. Robert Burns, "Tam O'Shanter," Alexandria Burns Club, accessed May 19, 2021, http://www.robertburns.org.uk/Assets/Poems_Songs/tamoshanter .htm. Public domain.
8. Charles Lamb, "Anger," All Poetry (website), accessed May 19, https://all poetry.com/poem/8527295-Anger-by-Charles-Lamb. Public domain.
9. Henri Nouwen, *Intimacy with God* (San Francisco: Harper & Row, 1969), 15. Nouwen wrote at a time when inclusive language as we use it was not common, and I have chosen not to change his language.

Chapter 12

1. Adnaan Bin Sallim, Andew Arjun Sayampanathan, Amit Cuttilan, Roger Chun-Man Ho, "Prevalence of Mental Health Disorders among Caregivers of Patients with Alzheimer Disease," *Journal of the American Medical Directors Association* 16, no. 12 (December 2015):1034–41.
2. Rainer Maria Rilke, *Letters to a Young Poet*, Goodreads, https://www .goodreads.com/quotes/523573-perhaps-everything-that-frightens-us-is -in-its-deepest-essence.
3. William D. Eisenhower, "Fearing God," *Christianity Today*, February 7, 1986, https://www.christianitytoday.com/ct/1986/february-7/fearing-god -those-who-have-never-trembled-from-head-to-toe.html.
4. Ann Lewin, "Stage Fright," in *Watching for the Kingfisher* (Norwich: Canterbury Press, 2014), 1. Used by permission.

Chapter 13

1. Sue Miller, *The Story of My Father* (New York: Alfred A. Knopf, 2003), 159–60.

2. Diane Ackerman, "The Accident," in *Origami Bridges: Poems* (New York: Harper Collins, 2002), 14. Used by permission.
3. Elie Wiesel, as told by Robert McAfee Brown in his Introduction to *The Trial of God* (New York: Schocken Books, 1995), xxv.

Chapter 14

1. Alzheimer's Association, "2018 Alzheimer's Disease Facts and Figures," https://www.alz.org/media/homeoffice/facts%20and%20figures/facts -and-figures.pdf.
2. Mandy Ma, Diana Dorstyn, Lynn Ward, and Shaun Prentice, "Alzheimer's Disease and Caregiving: A Meta-Analytic Review Comparing the Mental Health of Primary Carers to Controls," *Journal of Aging & Mental Health* 22, no. 11 (2018): 1–11, https://doi.org/10.1080/13607863.2017.1370689.
3. Sallim, "Prevalence of Mental Health Disorders," 1034–41; and S. Atteih et al., "Implications of Stroke for Caregiver Outcomes: Findings from the ASPIRE-S Study," *International Journal of Stroke* 10 (June 9, 2015): 918–23.
4. Sallim, "Prevalence of Mental Health Disorders," 1034–41.
5. Kenneth E. Covinsky et al., "Patient and Caregiver Characteristics Associated with Depression in Caregivers of Patients with Dementia," *Journal of General Internal Medicine* 12 (December 18, 2003): 1006–14, https://doi.org/10.1111/j.1525-1497.2003.30103.x.
6. For further reading: Laraine Winter et al., "Depressed Affect and Dimensions of Religiosity in Family Caregivers of Individuals with Dementia," *Journal of Religion and Health* 54, no. 4 (March 21, 2015): 1490–1502, https://doi.org/10.1007/s10943-015-0033-6; and R. S. Herbert et al., "Religious Beliefs and Practices Are Associated with Better Mental Health in Family Caregivers of Patients with Dementia: Findings from the REACH Study," *American Journal of Geriatric Psychiatry* 15, no. 4 (April 15, 2007): 292–300.
7. Theodore Roethke, "In a Dark Time," *The New Yorker*, January 16, 1960.
8. Edna St. Vincent Millay, "Ebb," in *Second April* (New York: Mitchell Kennerley, 1921). Public domain.
9. Henri Nouwen, *The Inner Voice of Love*, in *Beauty of the Beloved: A Henri J. M. Nouwen Anthology*, ed. Robert A. Jonas (London: Darton, Longman & Todd, 1999), 114.
10. Ralph Waldo Emerson, "Music," in *Poems* (Boston: Houghton, Mifflin and Company, 1904). Public domain.

Chapter 15

1. Alister McGrath, *Doubt in Perspective* (Leister, England: InterVarsity Press, 2007), 14.

2. Yehuda Amichai, "The Place Where We Are Right," in *The Selected Poetry of Yehuda Amichai*, trans. Chana Bloch and Stephen Mitchell, rev. ed. (Berkeley: University of California Press, 1996), 34.

3. Alfred Lord Tennyson, "From the Ancient Sage," Bartleby, https://www.bartleby.com/236/98.html. Public domain.

Chapter 16

1. Cheryl Richardson, *The Art of Extreme Self-Care* (Carlsbad, CA: Hay House, 2012), xii.

2. https://www.goodreads.com/quotes/551027-yesterday-i-was-clever-so-i-wanted-to-change-the.

3. Parker Palmer, *Let Your Life Speak* (San Francisco: Jossey-Bass, 1999), 30.

4. Bernard of Clairvaux, *Sermons on the Song of Songs,* vol. 1, ed. Kilian Walsh (Kalamazoo, MI: Cistercian Publications, 1976).

Chapter 17

1. Lewis B. Smedes, *The Art of Forgiving* (New York: Ballantine Books, 1997), 34.

2. Jonathan Sacks, *The Dignity of Difference* (London: Continuum, 2002), 182.

3. Martin Luther King Jr., in a sermon given at Dexter Avenue Baptist Church in Montgomery, AL, on November 17, 1957, https://kinginstitute.stanford.edu/king-papers/documents/loving-your-enemies-sermon-delivered-dexter-avenue-baptist-church.

Chapter 18

1. Elisabeth Kubler-Ross and David Kessler, *On Grief and Grieving: Finding the Meaning of Grief through the Five Stages of Loss* (New York: Scribner, 2005), 7.

2. Jude Weir, "Dementia Spousal Caregivers: An Exploration of Pre-Loss Grief Interventions to Mitigate Post-Loss Complicated Grief" (Master in Counseling thesis, City University of Seattle, May 2018).

3. Allison Lindauer and Theresa A. Harvath, "Pre-Death Grief in the Context of Dementia Caregiving: A Concept Analysis," *Journal of Advanced Nursing* (April 7, 2014), https://doi.org/10.1111/jan.12411.

4. Ibid.

5. Susan Roos, *Chronic Sorrow: A Living Loss* (New York: Routledge, 2002), 26.

6. Denise Levertov, "Talking to Grief," from *POEMS 1972–1982*, copyright ©1978 by Denise Levertov, page 111. Reprinted by permission of New Directions Publishing Corp. Used by permission.

7. Rumi, in *Mesnevi,* vol. 1, number 820–21. Translated from the Turkish by Ezgi Tiryaki.
8. Mark Johnson, excerpted from "In the Rain of Falling Petals," *Pilgrim Place News,* Claremont, CA, 2020, 4. Used by permission.
9. Nouwen, *Inner Voice of Love,* 114.

Chapter 19

1. S. Bruce Narramore, "Guilt: Where Theology and Psychology Meet," *Journal of Psychology and Theology* 2, no. 1 (December 1, 1974): 18–25.
2. Anne Wilson Schaef, *Women's Reality* (San Francisco: HarperSanFrancisco, 1992).
3. R. S. Thomas, "Emerging," in *Collected Poems: 1945–1990* (London: Orion Books, 1993), 263.
4. Huub Buijssen, *The Simplicity of Dementia: A Guide for Family and Carers* (London: Jessica Kingsley Publishers, 2005), 166.
5. Hafiz, "That Full, Fragrant Curl," in Ladinsky, *I Heard God Laughing,* 52.

Chapter 20

1. Tu Fu as quoted by Guy Gavriel Kay in *Under Heaven.* (New York: ROC, 2010), https://me.me/t/Guy%20Gavriel%20Kay-Under%20Heaven/quotes/NrpPtJbWMzki.
2. William Law, *A Serious Call to a Devout and Holy Life* (N.p., 1729).

Chapter 21

1. Leland R. Beaumont, "Hope: This Can All Turn Out for the Best," *Emotional Competency,* accessed April 3, 2015, http://www.emotional competency.com/hope.htm.
2. Wendy Duggleby et al., "Renewing Everyday Hope: The Hope Experience of Family Caregivers of Persons with Dementia," *Issues in Mental Health Nursing* 30, no. 8 (August 13, 2009): 514–21, https://www.tandfonline.com/doi/abs/10.1080/01612840802641727.
3. Henri Nouwen, quoted by ed. Robert A. Jonas, *Beauty of the Beloved: A Henri J. M. Nouwen Anthology* (London: Darton, Longman & Todd, 1999), 109, from "A Tribute to Henri Nouwen: 1932–1996," a Windborne video production.
4. Emily Dickinson, 254 " 'Hope' Is a Thing with Feathers—," in *The Poems of Emily Dickinson,* ed. Thomas H. Johnson (Cambridge, MA: The Belknap Press of Harvard University Press, Copyright © 1951, 1955, 1979, 1983 by the President and Fellows of Harvard College), 116.
5. Nouwen, in Jonas, *Beauty of the Beloved,* 110.

6. Vaclav Havel, *Disturbing the Peace*, trans. Paul Wilson (New York: Alfred A. Knopf, 1990), 181.

Chapter 22

1. Howard Gruetzner, *Alzheimer's: The Complete Guide for Families and Loved Ones,* 2nd ed. (New York: John Wiley and Sons, 1997), 181.
2. Joan Gershman, The Alzheimer Spouse, accessed July 2, 2014, http://thealzheimerspouse.com/old/blogs-2014.html.
3. https://quotecatalog.com/quote/lauren-oliver-i-wonder-if-thi-Y7AqY27.
4. A. S. J. Tessimond, "Not Love Perhaps," in *Not Love Perhaps* (London: Faber and Faber, 2015), https://www.independent.ie/lifestyle/not-love-perhaps-26831402.html. Used by permission.

Chapter 23

1. John Cacioppo, at the February 16, 2014, annual meeting of the American Association for the Advancement of Science in Chicago, in a seminar entitled "The Science of Resilient Aging." Information was accessed at Institute for Genomics and Systems Biology, January 25, 2011, http://www.igsb.org/news/psychologist-john-cacioppo-explains-why-loneliness-is-bad-for-your-health.
2. Ann Lewin, "Mothercare," in *Lifecycles*, ed. Elaine Graham and Margaret Halsey (London: Society for Promoting Christian Knowledge, 1993), 56.
3. Ella Wheeler Wilcox, excerpted from "Solitude," published in 1883. Accessed at Poetry Foundation, https://www.poetryfoundation.org/poems/45937/solitude-56d225aad9924. Public domain.
4. Dietrich Bonhoeffer, "Works," in *Letters and Papers from Prison* (Minneapolis, MN: Fortress, 2009), 238, Letter no. 89.
5. May Sarton, *A Journal of Solitude* (New York: W. W. Norton and Co., 1992).
6. Richard Rohr, "The Hidden Secret, Love: Week 2," Center for Action and Contemplation, January 4, 2016, https://cac.org/the-hidden-secret-2016-01-04.

Chapter 24

1. Alzheimer's Association, "Alzheimer's Disease Facts and Figures," 43.
2. David F. Maas, "Bible Verses about Resentment," Bible Tools (website), accessed May 20, 2021, https://www.bibletools.org/index.cfm/fuseaction/Topical.show/RTD/cgg/ID/332/Resentment.htm.
3. Donald L. Hicks, *Look into the Stillness* (Amelia, VA: Nature's Path, 2015), 43.
4. Br. Curtis Almquist, "Investing in Life," Society of Saint John the Evangelist, November 16, 2008, http://ssje.org/ssje/2008/11/16/investing-in-life.

Chapter 25

1. Jaroslav Vajda, "Now the Silence," in *The Hymnal 1982* (New York: The Church Hymnal Corporation, 1985), 333.
2. Milton Mayeroff, *On Caring* (New York: Perennial Library, 1972), 61.
3. Henri Nouwen, "All Is Grace," *Weavings* 7, no. 6 (November–December 1992), 38–41.
4. Henri Nouwen, *Intimacy* (San Francisco: Harper & Row, 1969), 58. Nouwen wrote at a time when inclusive language as we use it was not common, and I have chosen not to change his language.
5. Thomas Merton, in his final address as novice master at the Abbey of Gethsemani on August 20, 1965.
6. Henri Nouwen, *With Burning Hearts*, quoted in Jonas, *Beauty of the Beloved*, 117.
7. Hafiz, "I Am Determined," in Ladinsky, *I Heard God Laughing*, 44. Used by permission

Chapter 26

1. St. Julian of Norwich, in *Revelations of Divine Love*, the first book written in English by a woman, c. 1393.
2. Parker Palmer, "Heartbreak, Violence, and Hope for New Life," an interview on the podcast On Being, April 15, 2015, https://onbeing.org/blog/heartbreak-violence-and-hope-for-new-life.
3. Derek Walcott, "Love After Love," in *The Poetry of Derek Walcott 1948–2013* (New York: Farrar, Straus and Giroux, 2017), 227. Reprinted by permission from Farrar, Straus and Giroux.

Afterword

1. Thomas Centolella, " 'In the Evening We Shall Be Examined on Love,' " in *Lights & Mysteries* (Port Townsend, WA: Copper Canyon Press, 1995), 114. Copyright © 1995 by Thomas Centolella. Reprinted with the permission of The Permissions Company, LLC on behalf of Copper Canyon Press.

Acknowledgments

I give my wholehearted gratitude to all those who have helped in this writing by giving valuable feedback and interacting with the ideas shared here in this book, particularly Leslie Adams, Margy Davis-Mintun, Rita Goldenberg, Cherie Hylton, Dave Lutz, and Sally Wolfe.

I give my deepest thanks to Gladstone's Library in Wales, to Peter Francis and all the staff. The beauty, welcome, comfort, and silence of the library make it a perfect place to write.

I want to acknowledge the generosity of the following sources for their permission to use the poetry included in this volume:

Antonio Machado, *There Is No Road*, trans. by Mary Berg and Dennis Maloney. Buffalo, NY: White Pine Press, 2003.

"For a New Beginning" from *To Bless the Space Between Us: A Book Of Blessings* by John O'Donohue, copyright © 2008 by John O'Donohue. Used by permission of Doubleday, an imprint of the Knopf Doubleday Publishing Group, a division of Penguin Random House LLC. All rights reserved.

Wendell Berry, "Section X of Sabbaths, 1998," in *Given*. Washington, DC: Shoemaker Hoard, 2005. Permission granted through personal communication.

R. S. Thomas, excerpted from "Tell Us," in *Collected Later Poems: 1988–2000*. Northumberland, UK: Bloodaxe Books, 2004. Used by permission.

Hafiz, "We Should Talk About This Problem," in Daniel Ladinsky, *I Heard God Laughing*. New York: Penguin Books, 2006. Used by permission.

Rumi, "Let's Go Home," in John Moyne and Coleman Barks, *Open Secret: Versions of Rumi*. Putney, VT: Threshold Books, 1984. Used by permission.

"Eternal Spirit of the Living Christ." Words by Frank von Christierson © 1974 The Hymn Society (Admin. Hope Publishing Company, Carol Stream, IL 60188). All rights reserved. Used by permission.

"Disclosure" from *Watching for the Kingfisher* by Ann Lewin, copyright by Ann Lewin, 2009. Published by Canterbury Press. Used by permission.

Rumi, "The Guest House," in *Selected Poems by Rumi*, trans. Coleman Barks. London: Penguin Classics, 2004. Used by permission.

"Stage Fright" from *Watching for the Kingfisher*. Copyright by Ann Lewin, 2009. Published by Canterbury Press. Used by permission.

"The Accident" in *Origami Bridges* by Diane Ackerman. Copyright © 2002 by Diane Ackerman. Used by permission of HarperCollins Publishers.

Theodore Roethke, excerpted from "In a Dark Time," *The New Yorker*, January 16, 1960. Used by permission.

Yehuda Amichai, "The Place Where We Are Right," in *The Selected Poetry of Yehuda Amichai*, trans. Chana Bloch and Stephen Mitchell, rev. ed. Used by permission from University of California Press through Copyright Clearance Center.

Denise Levertov, "Talking to Grief" from *POEMS 1972–1982*, copyright ©1978 by Denise Levertov, page 111. Reprinted by permission of New Directions Publishing Corp.

Hafiz, excerpted from "That Full, Fragrant Curl," in Daniel Ladinsky, *I Heard God Laughing*. New York: Penguin Books, 2006. Used by permission of the translator.

Emily Dickinson. From *The Poems of Emily Dickinson*, edited by Thomas H. Johnson, Cambridge, Mass.: The Belknap Press of Harvard University Press, copyright © 1951, 1955, 1979, 1983 by the President and Fellows of Harvard College.

Hafiz, "I Am Determined," in Daniel Ladinsky, *I Heard God Laughing.* New York: Penguin Books, 2006. Used by permission of the translator.

Derek Walcott, "Love after Love" from *Sea Grapes by Derek Walcott.* Copyright 1976 by Derek Walcott. Reprinted by permission from Farrar, Straus and Giroux.

Thomas Centolella, "'In the evening we shall be examined on love'" from *Lights & Mysteries.* Copyright © 1995 by Thomas Centolella. Reprinted with the permission of The Permissions Company, LLC on behalf of Copper Canyon Press.

I have made every effort to trace copyright holders and to make correct acknowledgments. I apologize if any material has been included without permission or without appropriate acknowledgment, and would be glad to be told of anyone who has not been consulted.